Field of Brothers

NIALL PATTERSON

WITH SEAMUS MALONEY

www.**HERO**BOOKS.digital

HEROBOOKS

PUBLISHED BY HERO BOOKS
1 WOODVILLE GREEN
LUCAN
CO. DUBLIN
IRELAND

Hero Books is an imprint of Umbrella Publishing
First Published 2022
Copyright © Niall Patterson and Seamus Maloney 2022
All rights reserved

ISBN 9781910827482

Cover design and formatting: jessica@viitaladesign.com
Photographs: Sportsfile, John McIlwaine and the Patterson family collection

Dedication

My mum, my dad, and my family

Contents

« ACKNOWLEDGEMENTS »

I'M SURE IT wasn't easy with a family of seven, but mum looked after us all – and my granny Annie and my uncle Hughie, who were both diabetic. My mum was like a nurse to them as well as a daughter-in-law and sister-in-law, and also to my cousin Gerald Traynor, who died at the age of seven from a brain tumour.

Mum never complained and has always been the real rock of our family, like so many mothers are.

Dad was my hurling inspiration. I did my best so I could hear him say, 'Well done', which never happened because that's not the sort of man he was. He wouldn't say it because that was his way of keeping my feet on the ground. But I always knew he was proud of everything I achieved.

Johnny Coyle was my hurling mentor and treated me like a son. He was an unreal man who, like my dad, gave his life to Loughgiel.

Hurling is a team game and without all my teammates I wouldn't have been anything. I loved being part of those teams – when we were winning and when we weren't – standing shoulder-to-shoulder on the field and enjoying the craic off it.

I salute you all and thank you from the bottom of my heart.

The best day of my life was the day I married Naomi. Like my mum, she is the rock of our family and I couldn't be prouder of our children Rhiannon, Sharelle and Ashdyn.

Thank you to Seamus Maloney for his hard work and research in making this book happen, and thanks too to Seamus and Liam Hayes of Hero Books for even thinking I had a story to tell in the first place.

When Liam first approached me about this book, I told him I wasn't sure my story was worth it. He convinced me by reminding me that none of us get where we are by ourselves and this could be a chance to thank the people who have helped me along the way. So while these acknowledgements may be short, I hope the rest of these pages serve to acknowledge the countless people who have contributed in some way to my hurling, my music and my life.

Thank you all so much.

Niall Patterson
March 2022

◄◄◆►►

TO BE ABLE to help Niall tell his story over the past almost two years has been a privilege and a pleasure. Whether over the phone during lockdowns or at his home in Cloughmills, he brought to life characters from the worlds of hurling and music and made my job an easy one. During those visits to the Patterson house it proved a much more difficult job resisting the scones and other treats Niall's wife Naomi put in front of me with cups of tea, and I thank her for her hospitality.

Anyone writing a book would be lucky to have Liam Hayes as an editor, and he and his team at Hero Books have produced something I'm extremely proud to be associated with. My colleague Neil Loughran also deserves my thanks. A career as a literary agent awaits if the sportswriting doesn't work out.

Working with Niall was so enjoyable because it allowed me to relive some of my fondest childhood memories. I got to see Antrim play Kilkenny in Dundalk and win promotion against Dublin at Casement Park and light up Croke Park in 1989 because my dad Jimmy took me to those matches. I'll always be grateful and look forward to the next one.

I'm thankful for my wife Jennifer's patience and support every day I worked on this book – and every other day as well.

Seamus Maloney
March 2022

Prologue

Niall Patterson, appearing with his teammates from the
Antrim team that played in the All-Ireland final in 1989, is
honoured at half-time during the county senior final between
Cushendall and Dunloy at Ballycastle in 2019.

Saffron ties... Some of Niall's teammates from 1989 wear their saffron ties as they are honoured at half-time during the county senior final between Cushendall and Dunloy at Ballycastle in 2019. Top (from left) – Donal Armstrong, Olcan McFetridge and Dessie Donnelly. Middle – Brian Donnelly and Sambo McNaughton. Below (from left) – Paul McKillen, Ciaran Barr and Gary O'Kane.

Prologue

IT'S SEPTEMBER 2019 and we're out on the pitch in Ballycastle. Together again. We're all older, all slower, some a bit bigger, some with a few more grey hairs, some with fewer of any colour. And some of us are gone. We've lost our teammates, brothers Danny and James McNaughton, and Jim Nelson – the man who brought us together and took us to the biggest day in Antrim hurling history.

Thirty years after that day, the rest of us are here at half-time in the county final, suited and booted… saffron ties catching in the breeze coming off the Sea of Moyle.

We're being honoured by the Antrim County Board, which is nice of them, but the best thing about the day is to be back with these old friends.

I run into some of them all the time, some only on days like this. But whenever we do meet, we talk about the craic we had, the matches we won and lost, the times we lifted lumps out of each other with our clubs… and then went out a few days later, ready to give everything for each other and our county.

Before the match, we meet in the Marine Hotel for a meal and a catch-up – and to get ourselves wrapped in those ties. We're catching up all day, though when we get up to the ground the Cushendall and Dunloy boys amongst us are understandably distracted by what's happening on the pitch. I can't blame them.

If Loughgiel had been playing I'd be down in the middle of the crowd.

In that crowd we can all find more old friends, old teammates and opponents, people we've known for as long as we can remember... all part of what made all of us.

Some were my own heroes growing up. Some stood with me when Loughgiel became All-Ireland champions.

These boys in the saffron ties ran out onto Croke Park on the first Sunday in September, in 1989, after we had pushed for a decade to try to get Antrim hurling where we thought it could be.

I was the goalkeeper. I stood behind them, but I've had countless people standing behind me.

It's hard on a day like this not to meet someone you know, someone who played a part in your life. It's tough enough to do that at a league match in Dunloy or the Feis Cup in Armoy, never mind the county final in Ballycastle.

But, it's the same for me at a dinner dance in Cookstown or a festival in Donegal, or a marquee at an Irish bar in Portugal. Hurling and music have been the two constants in my life. Both have given me an awful lot, with good friends at the top of that list.

The match is being shown live on TG4, and they've asked me and our captain Ciaran Barr to come on and talk. As we make our way through the crowd, I see John Watt – The Singing Farmer – who wrote the song we recorded when we got to the final. Yes, we really did record a song... *Jim Nelson's Men*. I bring Ciaran over and introduce John, who's over the moon to meet him.

Through hurling and music, I've been lucky to travel all over Ireland – and much further – and I was even luckier that I was always part of a team, part of a band.

A Field of Brothers

I never did it alone.

PART ONE

'That Boy'll Never Be A Keeper!'

Niall with his mum Kathleen; brothers Anthony, Aidan and Jarlath; and sisters Katrina, Maggie and Ann. Anthony sadly died in 2014.

Liam McGarry holds the championship trophy aloft on the shoulders of Niall's father Neil.

Niall and his wife Naomi on holiday (right), and (below) the Patterson daughters, Rhiannon, Sharelle and Ashdyn.

Rhiannon makes it four generations of the family in one photo as the new-born is present with Niall, his mother Kathleen, and his grandmother Maggie.

« CHAPTER 1 »

LOUGHGIEL AND DUNLOY sit about five miles apart as the crow flies in north Antrim, two small villages whose names are known by hurling people wherever you go.

In between, you'll find Cloughmills.

There was a hurling club there in the 1940s – Patrick Og's – but it didn't last. Another, St Brigid's, was formed in 1992 and has survived and thrived, winning Antrim Junior and Intermediate Championships.

But, in between, if you were from Cloughmills and you wanted to play hurling there was Loughgiel and Dunloy.

Even though Cloughmills and Dunloy are the same parish, family ties almost always made your decision for you, though not all the time.

LOUGHGIEL HAVE HAD some fantastic hurlers over the years but, for my money, Seamus Richmond was 'pound for pound' the best of them all. He won championship medals in nearly every position... goalkeeper, centre-back, midfield, centre-forward, full-forward... he *played them all* and played them all to a high standard. Seamus lived about a half a mile from our house. His cousins Willie and Brendan lived up the same lane, but they hurled for Dunloy.

Despite being the 'other' parish, there's always been a strong affinity between Loughgiel and Cloughmills. In the Loughgiel team that won the All-Ireland title in 1983 the full-back PJ O'Mullan was from Cloughmills and in front of him centre-back Paddy McIlhatton, who was from Ballymena, lived in Cloughmills. Loughgiel's 2012 All-Ireland winning team also had two Cloughmills men in the full-back line... Neil McGarry and Paul Gillan, and another – Mark McFadden – in centrefield.

For me, it was all about family. My father Neil was a Cloughmills' man and he played for that Patrick Og's team. But when they folded, when it came to hurling, he became a Loughgiel man. He became a Shamrock.

So, I became a Shamrock too. Eventually.

The first hurling match I can remember was in Rasharkin, a few miles the other side of Dunloy, not far from the border with Derry. It was a carnival match and I was six or seven at the time, and staying at my granny's, my mother's mother. And my mother was born Kathleen McAllister. In Dunloy.

So, I was standing with my two aunts watching Dunloy play Loughgiel and, like them, I was shouting for Dunloy. I had no idea that my dad was there on the sideline with the Loughgiel team.

I couldn't tell you who won, but I was left with one clear memory of the day.

There was no fence around the field, nothing to separate the players from the supporters apart from a rope... not a very stern divide between the people watching on summer seats set up for the big match, and the blood and thunder going on on the pitch.

At one stage I got an extremely close-up view of the action.

A Dunloy forward was over near the line, right where we were standing, and the Loughgiel full-back came running out towards him, ready to plant one hand on his back and clear the ball away with the other.

But he missed, and instead of his hand landing on the Dunloy forward's back, it landed smack on the bridge of my nose and sent me flying. That was my first ever memory of a hurling match. It's maybe not surprising I can't remember who won.

But when it came time for me to move to the other side of that rope and play myself, there was never any question who it would be for.

MY DAD HAD been involved with Loughgiel – playing, coaching, managing... *everything* – long before I came along on January 2, 1962. A great GAA birthday. They used to joke that my dad held the birth certificate back a few days. That would have meant the match in Rasharkin was sometime around the late 60s, when Loughgiel boasted one of the greatest teams in the club's long, illustrious history, and one of the best Antrim has ever seen.

They won five county titles in six years and my father was involved behind the scenes in all of them. In the 10 years before that run started in 1966, Loughgiel were in the final seven times. Both times they won, in 1956 and '63, my dad was full-back. By 1963 he had actually retired, but Neil McMullan – who could well have been the man who sent me flying in Rasharkin – broke his leg and my dad stayed on another year, and won another county medal. I was too young to remember, but he played for Antrim too. I'm told he was a good full-back – hard to get around. Something every goalkeeper wants in the man standing in front of you.

I can't remember much from the big games those great Loughgiel teams played. I know I was at more of them, but the only county final I can recall being at was the last one, in 1971, when Loughgiel beat Glenariffe in Ballycastle, though I can't remember much more than that about it. Loughgiel wouldn't win another Antrim title for 11 years.

I can remember a bit more about that one.

Most of my memories of those great players weren't from matches, they were from training. My dad would bring me up to the pitch in the car and I'd sit and watch them... Johnny Coyle, Seamus Richmond, Seamus McMullan, Neil McMullan, Brendan McGarry. I'd be in awe of these legends. I finally got to play with Brendan and Seamus Richmond before they retired, and that was a dream come true.

The old dressing-room was like an air-raid shelter, but with a tin roof on it. There was no power, no lights. When it got dark the headlights of the cars around the pitch were turned on so they could keep training. Johnny Coyle was the goalkeeper and he was also my first coach, and when training was over my dad would say, 'Johnny, scoot that boy up home, we're going up to The Pound to pick this team'. Johnny had to leave me home almost every night.

The Pound was, and still is, The Pound Bar in Loughgiel, where they sat and picked the team for the following Sunday. Once it was picked it was put up in the window of McAdorey's shop on a Thursday night.

That's the way it was done for years, but by the time I started playing for the seniors things had changed because whenever the team was seen in the window of the shop it became the big topic of conversation in The Pound that night. It would be cut to ribbons or praised as a good team. Usually both. *Why's he not on? Why's he playing there?*

It got to the stage that putting the team up maybe caused a bit more trouble than it was worth, so even though it was still picked in The Pound on a Thursday night, it wasn't announced until the Sunday before the match. People would still give off – but now they could only do it for two or three hours, instead of two of three days.

I'M THE SECOND of seven... four boys and three girls. My brother Anthony, who died in 2014, was the oldest... then me, Aidan and Jarlath, twin sisters Maggie and Ann, and Katrina, the youngest.

Seven children was a smaller family than either my dad's or my mum's. There were eight Patterson siblings, and my dad had brothers Bobby, Hughie and Jim, along with sisters Annie, Mary, Nellie and Margaret.

Over in Dunloy, the McAllisters went one better. My mum was one of nine with Mary, Eileen, Philomena, Anne, Seamus and Charlie and twins... Madeleine and Elizabeth.

Unsurprisingly, hurling has run through all our lives. Anthony played reserve for Loughgiel, while Aidan got married and went down to Cushendall and hurled at intermediate level for them. Jarlath didn't play that much, although when Ballymena started a team, a teacher at school who was involved with them got him to play a bit at underage, but Charlie – everyone calls Jarlath 'Charlie' – is as big a Loughgiel supporter as you could find. He also lives in Dunloy and doesn't hide his affection for Loughgiel. Seamus McMullan, the Dunloy and Antrim great, once told him, 'Charlie, I don't mind you, because you hate us and tell us that to our faces. It's the boys who hate us and pat us on the back that I don't like'.

Maggie married Olcan Laverty, who I had many battles with when he played corner-forward for Ballycastle. He was a tough, *tough* competitor and carried a bit of a reputation, but I had a lot of time for him on the field. There were plenty of times he could have left the stick in on me and got away with it, but he didn't. And that was before he met my sister!

Ann married a Cushendall man, Johnny Regan, and Katrina married Jarlath Elliott from the famous Dunloy hurling family.

I'm sure my dad would have some craic if he was living now, with so much Dunloy, Ballycastle, and Cushendall in the family. I wonder how he'd feel if he was standing watching he grandwains playing against Loughgiel. I'm sure he'd want them to do well – even if he wouldn't say it. As much as he loved Loughgiel, he loved his family more.

He would have other counties to cheer on as well, because Aidan and his wife Nuala moved down to Cavan and their son Ronan played midfield for the county in an All-Ireland minor semi-final against Kerry. Ann and Johnny moved to Ballina and their son Sean also played for the county minors at Croke Park – and has been one of the main men for the Mayo hurlers for years as well.

MY DAD DIDN'T come from a hurling family at all, and when it came to our family he didn't push any of us into playing. If we *enjoyed* it, we enjoyed it and he'd then try to help us as much as he could. I started to show an interest, I think mainly through just going along to all those Loughgiel training sessions with him, and when my dad saw I wanted to play he'd send me out the back where we had a big shed with a corrugated iron door, about the size of a goal.

I'd batter a sponge ball against the door again and again, controlling it as it flew back at all sorts of different angles. That would have been good for any player, but it was especially good for someone who wanted to be a goalkeeper – and I *wanted* to be a goalkeeper. The reason? Johnny Coyle.

I couldn't have asked for a better first coach, and the things he taught me when I was nine or 10 years old stayed with me until the last day I picked up a stick.

There wasn't really such a thing as dedicated goalkeeper coaching back then, and Johnny just happened to be the coach of the whole team, but I learned so much from him.

Johnny had his wee quirks. He was known as 'Thick' – 'Thick' Johnny, and sometimes they called him Johnny 'Grunt'. That's just the way he was, but he had a heart of gold and was brilliant with me.

What Johnny taught me were the basics of goalkeeping... the building blocks. Things didn't get much more complicated than that back in those days, so it was up to a young boy to combine those basics with his own instincts and try to keep getting better.

Johnny kept goals in all seven of Loughgiel's championship winning teams from 1956 up to '71 – standing behind my dad for the last years of his playing career – and was his goalkeeper when Antrim won the All-Ireland Intermediate Championship when my dad was manager. He ended up being the first coach for a lot of the boys who went on to the win the All-Ireland for the club in 1983, and he didn't get enough credit for the part he played in that.

BEFORE HE STOPPED playing with Loughgiel, my dad was already involved as a selector with the county team. Antrim reached their first All-Ireland senior final in 1943, when they shocked Galway and Kilkenny at Corrigan Park in Belfast, before being put to the sword by Christy Ring's Cork in Croke Park. By the end of the 60s they were playing in the new Intermediate Championship.

So that became the big focus for the county team and in 1970, with my dad as the manager, they won Division Two of the National League before going on to beat Warwickshire in the All-Ireland intermediate final in Croke Park. Johnny Coyle was in goal and Seamus Richmond and Brendan McGarry were two of the star forwards.

It was a big win for Antrim – the first All-Ireland title the county had won – and my dad and his management team had left no stone unturned in trying to achieve it.

Along with his selector Frank Smyth, my dad went down to Cork to enlist Justin McCarthy's help before the first game of the championship against Galway. Justin should have been starring for Cork but he was still injured after a motorbike accident the previous year. My dad and Frank went down to the Munster final in Limerick and convinced Justin to come up and lend a hand.

They were building a new parochial house in Cloughmills at the time; all voluntary work, and my dad, who was a building contractor, was in charge. I was seven or eight and would have been hanging around, maybe carrying bricks up to the brickie, trying to help, probably getting in the way.

One day, my dad was taking Justin out to Loughgiel for training and he stopped for me to meet him. Justin signed a brand new hurling ball and gave it to me along with maybe half a crown. To be honest, I didn't have a clue who Justin McCarthy was at the time, so instead of the autographed ball being displayed in the house I just saw a *brand new* ball I could batter the life out of against the wall – which I did.

In 2004, Justin brought the Waterford team he'd just managed to the Munster title up to play Antrim in a challenge match in Ballycastle. The next day I just happened to be standing on the corner near the house as a car pulled up. Out gets Justin McCarthy with the Munster Championship cup. He knew my dad had died and he hadn't seen my mum since way back when he was involved with Antrim, so he was up to see her.

I took him across the street, because the fella who has the pub there, Tony O'Hanlon, is from Waterford. Dan Shanahan and Tony Browne were with him too and they were nice lads. There's a photo of Justin and my mother standing in our house in Cloughmills with the Munster cup.

He had no need to do it but he wanted to do it for her. I thought the world of him for that.

SO MANY OF my earliest memories are of being with my dad, either of going down to hurling training with him, hanging around the building sites where he was contractor, or sailing about with him all over the place when he was involved in a wholesale spirits business. When he was a contractor, the house always seemed to have the men working for him in and out of it as mammy made them cups of tea.

A lot of the houses in front of the chapel in Cloughmills were built by my dad and his men, and with our house right there as well I would always be around the place. One the workers, Dan McGurk, let me follow him about and maybe hand him the odd brick or whatever. I'll always remember Dan falling off one of the roofs when I was young. Thankfully, he was fine.

Everyone who remembers him says my dad was a great tradesman, but I'm told that he gave up the building work so he could give more time to the hurling – something that doesn't surprise me one bit.

My uncle Hughie ran the shop on the corner, which was very much a family business and when I'd come in from school I'd be out the back with my dad in the shed, weighing the loose potatoes to be bagged up and sold in the shop.

One of his friends, Denny Molloy used to own a pub out on the main road between Ballymena and Ballymoney, and they started a wholesale spirits business together. They expanded from drink to the likes of pool tables and other bar supplies that came over from Scotland in what, to me at that time, seemed like the biggest lorry in the world.

That meant my dad started travelling all over the north for sales, and during the summer holidays I would go with him. Over to Tyrone and Derry, and up to the north coast… that's how I spent a large part of my summers before I was a teenager. At the time it was just what I did, and it was only years later that I realised how close I was to him, between the hours spent sitting next to him as he drove around with work and the hours we spent together with hurling.

I ALWAYS ENJOYED the classroom, and when it came time to leave primary school I managed to pass my 11-plus and went to St Louis', the grammar school in Ballymena. I was happy there too, and when I was in first year, Seamus McCamphill, whose brother PJ would end up being chaplain to the Antrim team in 1989, was the PE teacher and had me playing in goal for the third year team. I don't remember us winning much, if anything, but we had a great time playing together. There were boys from Loughgiel, Dunloy and other clubs who were big rivals playing, but Seamus would make sure we remembered that we were schoolmates and that we had to work together for the team.

Seamus was playing for Dunloy against Loughgiel in a Feis Cup match one day, when all hell broke loose. Seamus just walked off the field and into the dressing-room – he didn't want to be involved in that sort of thing. The next day at school, we all kept at him going… 'You're yella, sir!' But when you grow up, you realise he was one hundred percent right.

Even when I was younger, I wasn't interested in the nastiness you can get between club rivals. Of course, I wanted to beat them, but with so many Dunloy relations I could hardly view them as deadly enemies.

I used to stay at my granny's in Dunloy during the holidays, and I got some stick from Dunloy boys and I gave some back, but it was all good banter when we were growing up. I was already on the Loughgiel senior team when I was a minor and when I'd walk down from the Dunloy pitch to my granny's house after a minor match her next-door neighbour, Margaret, would be at me: 'You shouldn't be playing, Patterson… you're playing senior, and it's not right that you're playing among them wains'.

If my aunt Anne was in my granny's house the banter would keep going, but I always enjoyed it. I'd go into my granny's and maybe my aunt Anne would be there and we'd have the craic about the matches. Even though she was a Dunloy woman, my granny always backed me. My aunt Anne was harder to convince.

She married Eamonn Downey from Lavey in Derry and her son Emmet played for Lavey, but when they came up against Dunloy in the Ulster Championship she was shouting for Dunloy – with her son playing for the other team.

When I was playing minors against Dunloy, a friend I worked with in the shirt factory, Paddy McQuillan, was playing corner-forward for them. When he bent down to tie his lace I hit him a slap on the backside, with the stick, just carrying on. Next thing I knew, the referee was running in to book me and Paddy had to plead my case and explain we were just bantering like we always did.

Sometimes the rivalry did get the better of me. When I was a teenager, Loughgiel were playing Dunloy in the championship and were losing by 14 points at the start of the second-half. I was sitting on the bonnet of the car and an old man from Cloughmills walked past and poked me in the side with his walking stick.

'Where's the Shamrocks now?' I didn't tell him where the Shamrocks were, but I told him where to go…and didn't hold back.

Next thing I knew, my mum had gotten out of the car and hit me the most merciless slap. I think it was for my language rather than because she was a Dunloy woman.

Mammy used to go to all the matches and sat in the car with Johnny Coyle's wife Margaret, while I was standing outside at the wire. Even after I took over from Johnny, Margaret would come and sit in mammy's car, and watch. Both of them sitting there, playing every ball.

Even with my dad being involved with Loughgiel, mammy remained a Dunloy supporter until one match when Seamus Richmond was playing against Dunloy and he was hit one of the most brutal slaps I've ever seen on a hurling field. It nearly opened him from ear to ear and he ended up in hospital.

Seamus was a great family friend – I ended up playing in bands with him for a decade. When Seamus was hit like that, mammy said, 'That's it!'

She never shouted for Dunloy again.

I WAS IN St Louis' for three years, but I had got in with a crowd of boys who weren't all that interested in doing work and I was following suit. I was doing well enough but my parents reckoned I was capable of more and that maybe a change of scene would help.

The rest of our family went to St Patrick's High School in Ballymena, so it was decided that I'd do the same.

In my first couple of days I got a message to come in and see the head teacher Mr McCrackan, and he sat me down and read me the riot act. 'You've got six weeks, Patterson!' he told me. 'It seems you've got brains to burn, but you're lazy. You'll not be lazy here.'

That was me told, and I had to knuckle down. I probably learned more in St Pat's in my first year there than in my three at St Louis'. Something just clicked with me and I really took to it. The following year, I was put onto the senior committee at school; the pupils who would sit down and have meetings with the teachers. I got on well at St Pat's, and really enjoyed my time there. I enjoyed St Louis' too and the teachers were great, but I just found they did it a different way at St Pat's that suited me better and I got an awful lot out of my last two years at school there.

MY FIRST JOB after leaving school was with a glazier, Tom McNulty. The McNultys and our family were close and my sisters and Tom's daughters ran about together when they were children. I did about a year with Tom, putting windows into houses, and then a job came up in the local shirt factory in Cloughmills.

The factory employed half the village, as well as half of Loughgiel, Dunloy, Armoy... people from all over the area. In the factory we were making shirts and it honestly wasn't work I was particularly interested in. It was a just a job.

I had been playing music since I was 14, and that's really what I wanted to do for a living. But I wanted to play hurling as well and there was no way I could try to be a full-time musician and play hurling at the same time. There were only so many evenings and weekends to go around. So, the factory job was steady work to pay the bills.

Dominic McKinley – 'Woody' – was working in the factory at that time as well. We played on underage teams together right the way through with Loughgiel, and made our senior debuts for Antrim on the same day against Kilkenny in Nowlan Park.

He was always the biggest man for stirring things. He did it at work, he did it with hurling... he did it everywhere. He'd make the snowballs, set them up, let someone else throw them and then he'd sit back and enjoy the results. A deadly man.

On the pitch he was a great leader and motivator – team talks from 'Woody' were fantastic. He's the sort of boy who would eat the face off you if he thought you *needed* it, and put the arm round you if he thought you *needed* it. He was very similar to my dad in that way. It was no surprise to me when he became a manager and a coach with Antrim and Derry, and a history-making one with the Slaughtneil camogs, who won three All-Ireland senior titles in-a-row. He always had that way about him, even when he was just one of the 15 players.

When he played, he could stop anybody. He was a real spoiler; we could depend on 'Woody' to stand next to the opposition's danger man and more often than not keep him in check. Christy Heffernan was doing great things for Kilkenny in the 80s, for instance, but I think he scored a point, maybe, in four games against 'Woody'. Liam Fennelly was the new forward star for Kilkenny when we made our debuts and 'Woody' came on in the second-half and never let him hit a ball in his very first county match. He stuck to an opponent like glue.

It was 'Woody' who gave me a nickname which – thankfully – didn't stick, or at least didn't become as famous as some of the other nicknames we had in the Antrim team that reached the All-Ireland final. If it seemed like just about everybody on that team had a nickname, that's because it's true. It's not really surprising that these names caught the imagination of commentators when we started making some waves.

I had no idea where half the boys got their nicknames, but that was just what everyone called them. I didn't know until I read his book that Terence McNaughton's nickname 'Sambo' came from the TV programme *Love Thy Neighbour* and was a racist insult aimed at one of the characters. In the more than 40 years I've known him, I've never called him Terence in my life.

The same goes for Olcan McFetridge, Terence Donnelly, Aidan McCarry and Dominic McKinley. They'll never be anything but 'Cloot', 'Hippy', 'Beaver' and 'Woody' to me.

'Woody' christened me 'Stavros', which was the name of Telly Savalas' brother in the TV show *Kojak*. It was the big bushy head of hair that did it. Maybe it was because they stopped making *Kojak* that the nickname didn't become as famous as the others. When we were getting more attention, I was still just 'Niall'... sometimes, the obvious 'Big Niall'.

Towards the end my career I'd get 'Neilly' up in Belfast, which my dad used to get too with city folk. I didn't mind that.

CLOUGHMILLS WAS A great wee village to grow up in.

I loved it, and never wanted to leave. Most of the friends I grew up with still live here. We did all the things wee boys do growing up. We played football together anywhere we could. We used to go up into the school field, which is behind where I live now… sneak in there and kick about the football. You weren't allowed to go into it, and we used to get hunted all the time, but that was all part of the fun.

If we were chased out of there, we'd go over to a set of garages and use the garage doors for goals, either kicking the football or playing hurling. There's a big hill that we used to call 'the mountain' – because that's what it looked like to us – and we'd run about there or ride our bikes.

Compared to Loughgiel and Dunloy, Cloughmills was much more of a mixed village – and still is. Dunloy and Loughgiel are almost exclusively Catholic, whereas Cloughmills is mainly Protestant, but my experience was always a good one. We all got on really well and still do. It was a great time to be growing up. We all ran about together and those friendships are still there to this day.

When it came to sport, as I've said my dad was all about hurling, but I loved to play football too. I played gaelic with Glenravel – Loughgiel didn't have a team and Dunloy was hardly an option. I kept goals for them at minor level for a couple of years. We played soccer too, either in those kickabouts with friends in front of the garage doors, with the factory team that played in its own competition or with the Cloughmills team in the competitive local league.

'Woody' played too, and 'Cloot' was a very good soccer player as well and played with Armoy against Glentoran in the Irish Cup. I ended up stopping because of my dad. He didn't give me an ultimatum or anything like that, he just convinced me that it was too big a risk to be playing soccer, where we could get injured and be missing for the hurling.

Most weekends, I was playing a soccer match on a Saturday, then a hurling match on a Sunday, and although I'd have preferred to keep playing both, my dad won me over. As usual, he was probably right, even if I didn't see it at the time.

When I did stop playing soccer, I felt that it took a little something away from my hurling because it helped me figure out my angles a bit better, especially when coming out to close down a forward heading for goal. But, I suppose, I'd think about it differently if one of those times playing soccer I'd gone over on my ankle and not been fit to play hurling.

That was my dad's big fear, especially when I started to play with the county. He wasn't the type who was against soccer in principle, and he would never admit it but he liked to watch it if there was a match on the TV. It was just that he didn't want me doing anything that might come at the expense of hurling.

What was the point in working your way onto the county team and taking your chance only for it to be gone because you had played a game of soccer on a Saturday afternoon?

Hard to argue against that!

Of course, my dad could say that to me, but he let the other boys get on with it. He was never going to make any big statements about what boys could and couldn't do. There were times 'Woody' was travelling with us on the Saturday before a county game and my dad would be waiting on him to get back from his soccer match. But he never said a word. He knew, in an amateur game, that he couldn't dictate to someone what they could and couldn't play. Jim Nelson had the same attitude.

No one was going off to play soccer the day before a championship match or anything, but when we were down in Division Two of the National League boys would take a chance... live their lives, and if they got hurt, they got hurt! You might be read the riot act for it, but you wouldn't be dropped off the panel or anything like that.

Jim and my dad knew the importance of having happy players in the panel, and the easiest way to have happy players is to treat them like adults, not children. Although, when one of the members of that same panel actually is one of your children, it's a lot easier to convince them they maybe should give up playing soccer on a Saturday afternoon.

MY UNCLE HUGHIE was in the navy, and after he came out my granny bought the building down in front of the chapel that used to be the parochial house, as well as the parochial hall behind it. As well as becoming our home, some of the building was turned into a café and one of the rooms was made into a shop which became my uncle Hughie's – HN Patterson for Hugh Nevin Patterson.

Everybody would come in to hear Hughie's stories, and he was full of them. Just how many were actually true, you never knew. Hughie and some of the other real characters from the village would sit down on the corner outside the shop and tell their stories. That was Hughie's Corner.

Even while I was in the factory, I still helped out and worked quite a bit in the shop. Eventually I came in full-time and when Hughie retired, I took it over. But I never changed the name. When it became one of the most famous corner shops in Ireland – as the Dublin media seemed to be up every day leading up to the 1989 All-Ireland final – the sign above the door still said... HN Patterson.

When I closed down the shop, Anthony's wife and daughter took it on as a café and called it Hughie's. Now it's Aoife Quinn Hairdressing – Aoife is my niece, Maggie and Olcan's daughter.

More than 80 years after my granny bought it, it's still in the family.

« CHAPTER 2 »

MY FIRST HURLING stick wasn't really my own. When you were an under-12 back then you didn't get your own stick.

A potato bag would be brought out and emptied onto the field.

'There's the sticks lads… lift one and away you go!'

When you were finished, you'd put it back in the bag.

The next night you might pick up the same stick again, or you probably wouldn't. When you were that age, that's the way it was.

When I got a bit older, I'd go out the back to the shed where my dad had stick after stick hanging in the rafters. I'd pick out a couple of those sticks, fiddle with them so they felt right, and that was me *ready*.

When I was a minor, I hit the ball further than I ever did when I was senior, and that was thanks to my stick. Liam Laverty, who hurled for Loughgiel at corner-back when I came onto the senior team, had a stick made for him by Jimmy Darragh from Kilrea, just over the county border in Derry. But it was too heavy for Liam and he just he couldn't work with it. So, I swapped a stick with him and, all of a sudden, my puckouts were going a mile.

There was great whip to the stick. It was heavy at the heel and it seemed to send the ball… *forever*. I lost maybe 20 yards off my pucking out when I broke that stick and it nearly *broke* my heart. I went over to Jimmy Darragh to see if he could make me one the same.

He made me four different sticks but none of them were the same. Nothing else was like it.

So, it was back to the shed to pick one from the rafters. It was a Randall, from Wexford, with the toe broken off it. It had a thick handle on it, something I never liked, so I scoped it down with a bit of glass – that's something my dad always did and I picked up that habit from him – to get it to suit my hand.

It felt good after that, but the toe was missing and it was only half a stick. Joe Scullion was a teammate who started fixing and making sticks as a hobby and then turned it into a business that his sons run today. I took it down to Joe and he put a new toe on it for me. There was a nice sort of whip in it; my dad must have had it well-treated with linseed oil, and I used that for pucking out the ball.

But it still didn't feel just right, so I took it back down to Joe and asked him if he could put a bit of weight in it. Joe drilled three holes in the bottom of it and poured three ounces of lead into the holes and plugged it up with wee dowelling rods.

I worked with it and it wasn't right.

It felt too heavy, so we took two ounces out of it again. That stick lifted from the shed out the back, with a handle scoped down with a piece of glass, a new toe and an ounce of lead in the heel became my pucking out stick for my whole career.

'THAT BOY'LL NEVER BE A GOALKEEPER!'

I can still hear those words, nearly 50 years later.

In 1974 we reached the Antrim Feile final. No one came near us in north Antrim and when we went to play the south Antrim – in other words, Belfast – champions in the county final we thought we'd have a great chance of winning. The south Antrim champions that year were Commedagh, which was supposed to be an amalgamation of St John's and one or two other clubs in the city, but I think it was closer to being the pick of Belfast.

I was still under-12, and playing for the under-14s, and overall we were a pretty young team. We'd never seen anything like these boys from Belfast. We were only bits of wains, but they were coming out with what to us looked like full-grown moustaches and big long sideburns. It was like men against boys. And we took a really bad beating – 12-11 to 1-1. I let in six of them. I think I kicked one in myself.

I was traumatised. I was taken off at half-time; they put Seamus McNaughton

30

in goals and he didn't fare a lot better, so they brought Seamus out and put the full-back in. Nothing made any difference.

That match had a big bearing on my career. Hearing that man say I'd never be a goalkeeper hurt me. I wanted to prove that I could be a goalkeeper. Johnny Coyle was my hero. I wanted to be like him.

I didn't just want to be a goalkeeper... I wanted to be the Loughgiel goalkeeper.

I wonder what that fella was thinking nine years later when he watched six of the boys from that team – Aidan McNaughton, Robin Clarke, Martin Coyle, Paddy Carey, and even two of the boys who picked all those balls out of the net, Seamus McNaughton and myself – help our club win the All-Ireland title.

SOME OF THOSE games we played together as we grew up are clearer in my memory than many All-Ireland Championship matches in Croke Park that I played with Antrim.

The McMullan Cup is the North Antrim Under-16 Championship and is a big deal for any young hurler. The fact it was always played before the Feis Cup final – a big occasion with a big crowd – made it even bigger.

Every single year, Ballycastle seemed to beat us in the final. No matter how well we played, no matter how well we thought we were going, Ballycastle always seemed to beat us in the final. So, when another final came around and Ballycastle were there waiting for us, they were hot favourites to beat us again. Sean Carey – 'Tinkle' – who would go on to play corner-back in front of me on the All-Ireland team, was taking the team and he had us motivated something serious. *We couldn't let Ballycastle beat us again.* This really was a big deal.

A big part of the reason Ballycastle kept beating us was Brian Donnelly. Brian would go straight onto the county senior team as a teenager and, instantly, was one of the big players on the team. He then went on to be one the best players in the country for 10 years. So, you can imagine what he like when he was 16. He was virtually unstoppable.

I think we were maybe two or three points up with about 10 or 15 minutes left and Brian came tearing through the defence and drove the ball at the goal. It hit me on the shoulder and I managed to get it into my hand and clear it as far away as I could.

But Brian kept coming!

I held up the stick and… CRACK… it broke clean across his chest. But it wasn't my stick.

The Loughgiel seniors were playing the Feis Cup final that day and Johnny Coyle had lent me a brand new goalkeeper's stick for the McMullan Cup final – the first time I had ever used a goalkeeper's stick. And now it was sitting in a couple of pieces thanks to the full force of Brian Donnelly.

Johnny was sitting behind the goals in his car and I turned round and shouted: 'SORRY JOHNNY… I BROKE YOUR STICK!

'NEVER WORRY ABOUT THE STICK!'

And I won my McMullan Cup.

It was the same at minor level. Brian and Ballycastle kept getting the better of us and when we finally made the county final in 1979, things went wrong against Rossa. We were beating them well enough but when we came out after half-time the Rossa mentors were all around the referee, complaining about something. We never got a free in the second-half… they got a late penalty and beat us by a point.

So, 1980 was my last chance. In the semi-final we played St John's and we were two points up with maybe two minutes to go. They got a penalty… and I had Aidan McNaughton to my left… and Dominic McMullan to my right.

Shane Caldwell flicked the ball up and hit an unmerciful shot.

Dominic stopped it… and the ball landed at my feet. I shouted to the two boys to… 'LEAVE IT!' I scooped it up and, as the ball rose from the ground, I could see a St John's man running in on top of me.

I went to catch it in my hand and pull it into my chest but, somehow, I managed to hand-pass it into the net. Dominic McMullan called me everything under the sun. I've never hit a ball as far in my life as I did for that puckout. It dropped just short of the square, into Paddy Carey's hand and he buried it into the net. Their goalkeeper tried a quick puckout, but Sean Coyle caught it, put it over the bar and we were in the county final.

We went on to beat Rossa in that final and I won my Minor Championship.

I ALWAYS PLAYED in goals for Loughgiel.

It suited me, not just because of my size, but because I naturally picked up the skills and awareness I needed pretty quickly – and when you're young and can puck the ball as far as I could, you're going to be in goals.

I did play centre-forward on the school team at St Pat's for some of the most memorable matches I ever played. We played in the Vocational Schools' Championship and St Pat's had never won it before. We got to the semi-final, where we were playing Our Lady of Lourdes, Ballymoney, whose team was full of Loughgiel and Dunloy boys.

There were a few Loughgiel boys on the St Pat's team as well – Seamus McNaughton and Martin Coyle, who would play with me on the All-Ireland team. They were there, as well as Sean Coyle and PJ McKillop. The rest would have been from junior clubs like Ballymena and Ahoghill. We had a fella, Tony McCall, who was a schoolboy soccer international and went on to have a great career in the Irish League. He used to run with the ball on the stick… then kick it. We were a mixture like that, but we worked hard for each other.

We were three points down against Ballymoney with about a minute left, and I got the ball and was pulled down going through. Danny McMullan, who would coach our All-Ireland winning team in Loughgiel, was a teacher in Ballymoney and was refereeing the match. So, I stood on the '21' and Danny came out to me with the ball.

'Time's up!' he announced.

'What do you mean?'

He told me time was up and the ball had to go directly into the net.

'If it deflects off a stick, it doesn't count!'

There weren't any nets in the goals and Brendan McGarry, who would be in that All-Ireland side too and was another teacher in Ballymoney, stood behind the goals for the penalty. I threw it up… and buried it.

Wide ball.

I lost it, and started cursing.

Joe McGurk was our PE teacher and he was taking the team, and he chastised me for my foul-mouthed language.

'Ask Brendan Dooey! He ducked and it near took the head of him!'

Brendan, who was standing on the line admitted it was goal. So that goal got us a replay back at our place in Ballymena. We had two pitches, an all-weather pitch and a grass pitch, and we put them on the all-weather pitch because they'd never played on it before and we knew they wouldn't work with it. Half the school must have been out watching. We destroyed them.

We went on to beat St Aloysius' of Cushendall in the final to win the school's first ever championship. I was playing centre-forward again and it wasn't until years later that I found out that the two boys playing centre-back for Cushendall that day, and who marked me at various stages in the match, were 'Sambo' and James McNaughton, who I'd be running out onto Croke Park alongside in an All-Ireland final.

ANTRIM HAD STARTED to enter their minor team in the Leinster Championship in the late-70s to try to get younger hurlers used to playing against southern teams; so when they made the step up to senior level it wouldn't be the shock to the system that a lot of Ulster teams seemed to experience when they went down south.

They didn't want the minors to get that shock either, so when we were under-16 they had a development team go down to Leinster and play minor teams from Laois and Dublin. We were meant to be playing Dublin in Croke Park before the Antrim seniors – and the Dublin footballers, who were All-Ireland champions at the time, were supposed to be playing in a challenge match there as well. But it was a really wet day, and they moved our match to a school pitch.

But they still took us to Croke Park for the senior matches, and before the games started, they let us out onto the pitch. I'd never been to Croke Park before, never mind walk on the pitch. The place was completely empty, but I stood there on the most famous turf in the country and the hairs stood on the back of my neck. It just looked… *enormous*.

The Antrim seniors won that day. After the match, I was standing where the Dublin footballers were coming out before their game. There I am, when Jimmy Keaveney comes out onto the pitch right in front of me. I couldn't believe I was standing so close to this man who I'd only ever seen on TV.

I was like a child in a sweet shop, and that feeling of awe when meeting great players from other counties has never left me. Maybe that was a flaw when I was playing, maybe I shouldn't have been like that. But that's just the way I am.

ANTRIM HAD ALREADY played in Leinster for couple of years and showed that they could hold their own by the time our team went down to play Dublin in the first round in 1979. But it was still reckoned to be a big surprise when Paddy

Carey scored a couple of goals and we beat them easily at Croke Park.

That same weekend, Down had an even easier win against Westmeath, which meant there would definitely be an Ulster team in the Leinster minor final. We went back to Croke Park for the semi-final and completely dominated Down. The game was over long before the end, and with Down only scoring 1-1, I had very little to do.

It must have been to entertain myself that, in the second-half, I lifted one of the plastic balls that we used to have for training and which I spotted sitting beside the goals. There was a bit of a breeze behind me.

I thought there'd be no harm in seeing just how far I could hit this thing. I was still using the stick I had gotten from Liam Laverty and I put all of it through this wee light plastic ball. It probably wouldn't have counted, but it didn't matter as I put it wide anyway.

There was a fair bit of excitement in the county about reaching the final. Big days like that were still few and far between for Antrim. Playing Kilkenny in a Leinster final, before the senior decider at Croke Park, generated a bit of a buzz. We got a brand new rig for the match – white jerseys with saffron, and black stripes down the sleeve. We were given these the night before in the hotel… and Ger Rogan was so impressed with it, he put it on and went to bed in it.

We knew we were up against it playing Kilkenny, but our chances got even slimmer thanks to the sort of thing the Antrim County Board seemed to be expert at through many of my years playing – and for a good few years after.

They scheduled a round of Minor Championship matches for the week before the Leinster final, and our captain Terence Barton and Ciaran Donnelly both got themselves sent off against Loughgiel. They were suspended for the Leinster final. I can't remember what they did, but it wouldn't have been like Terence, who was a very clean hurler, and seriously talented.

A couple of years later in an under-21 All-Ireland semi-final against Kilkenny, I pucked a ball out on top of Terence and he stepped under it and doubled it straight over the bar.

Ciaran was a fine hurler too but, knowing him, I doubt he was sent off for shaking hands. Ciaran was the sort who would have taken the head off your shoulders and then carried you off the pitch when the match was over. Hard, tough, but a real gentleman, and a lovely fella.

Even if Terence and Ciaran had been able to play, they probably wouldn't have made much difference. When we got to Croke Park, Kilkenny showed us no mercy. Conditions were perfect… and they destroyed us.

It was the biggest game any of us had ever played, on the biggest stage. By the time the match was over there were nearly 30,000 people in Croke Park, in to watch the Kilkenny and Wexford seniors play their final.

There wasn't much of a crowd when we started, and there still wasn't much of a crowd in by the time the match was effectively over.

A mix-up in the defence let them score their first goal after five minutes and even though we were hurling well enough and holding our own for a big part of the match – Brian Donnelly and Liam Quinn had great games that day – every time we made a mistake, they just pounced on it.

They scored three more goals… we were four goals down at half-time.

Eamonn Mullan scored a goal early in the second-half but that was as good as it got for us. Kilkenny got another goal and the rest of the match was just played out. In the end we lost by 19 points.

My clearest memory of that final is how impressed I was with Michael Walsh, who was playing in goals for Kilkenny. His dad Ollie was a legendary Kilkenny goalkeeper and Michael reminded me of Noel Skehan – a 'keeper with a bit of flash, who would make a save and then carry the ball out 40 yards.

Not – unsurprisingly – something that was ever part of my game.

IT'S EASY TO say these things in hindsight, but we went into the 1980 Minor Championship convinced that we would win the All-Ireland. That might sound especially strange for an Antrim hurling team, particularly one that had been beaten so badly by Kilkenny the year before, but we knew that on our day we were more than a match for anyone.

We had lost some great players from the year before who were over age, like Brian Donnelly, Terence Barton and Ger Rogan, but there was a good core of players still there and more who came up to take their chance. Still, Antrim wouldn't be *Antrim* without some sort of drama. Ballycastle didn't send any players to the minors that year, and one of those was 'Cloot', who was playing with Ballycastle that season, as Armoy didn't have a minor team. Like Brian Donnelly, 'Cloot' was already the finished article when he was a minor.

But, even with those boys missing, we were confident, and a lot of that came from the players we had in our team – especially the ones from Belfast. Aidan McNaughton was our captain and a confident hurler, but he had *nothing* on those Belfast boys.

Frank Keenan from Gort na Mona, Seanie Quinn, Brendan Trainor from Rossa, Mickey Carlin and Collie Donnelly from St John's were all confident guys and that spread through the whole team. Mickey and Collie were both on that Commedagh team, who gave us the hammering in the Feile final. Collie, who'd later become the county chairman, was the cockiest wee so-and-so you ever saw on a hurling pitch.

He wasn't the height of two daisies, but boy could he play!

Our confidence nearly cost us in the first round against Laois, when we hung on to win by a point after being well ahead at half-time thanks to a strong breeze. We only managed a point in the second-half but did enough to earn another shot at Kilkenny in the quarter-final.

However confident we might have been, I doubt it compared to how confident Kilkenny were before playing us in Nowlan Park. They were at home – where they never lost. They hadn't been beaten in the Leinster Championship in 10 years, and were playing a team they had hammered the previous year.

But we headed down knowing we could surprise them.

One reason was that when we saw the team, Michael Walsh, whose dad Ollie was the manager, was picked at centre-forward instead of in goals, where he had played against us the year before. We wondered if Kilkenny maybe weren't as strong as they could be if they had to bring him out the field?

We nearly had to change our goalkeeper from the year before as well, all thanks to a visit to a fairground the night before the match. We were passing the time, and I was sitting on a motorbike that was attached to a merry-go-round with hobby-horses and that sort of thing. All of a sudden, it took off at serious speed and I was hanging on for grim death. I was half-on and half-off… and they couldn't get the thing stopped.

When they finally got it stopped and I could finally let go, my arm was killing me. I had managed to twinge something and didn't know if I would be fit to play the next day. Thankfully, a night's sleep and no more merry-go-rounds meant it was all right.

If Kilkenny didn't think they were going to be in a match, we soon let them know about it. We started well and didn't let them settle. All the things we wanted to do the year before against them in Croke Park, we were finally doing in Nowlan Park.

We kept the ball moving, got it into our full-forwards as quickly as we could… and Seanie Quinn got a goal that had us four points up at half-time. But that four-point advantage would have been gone in the blink of an eye if it hadn't been for our corner-back Vincent Trainor.

During that first-half, Vincent's man got the ball and managed to get past him and was bearing down on me. He was clean through and as I came off my line, he dropped the ball and hit it off the ground. I slid and tried to make myself as big as possible – I was big enough anyway. But, as I went down to spread myself, hoping the ball would hit me, he put it over me.

As I kept sliding out, I looked over my shoulder to see where the ball was going. It was heading for the net, but Vincent must have sprouted wings. He followed his man on through and had gone past me as I came out. He kept running and flicked the ball away, just as it was about to go over the line. Our full-back Damian Murray got the ball to Mickey Carlin, who hand-passed it to Collie Donnelly, who stuck the ball over the bar.

A four-point swing, all of it while I was lying on the ground, and thanks to Vincent Trainor coming out of nowhere.

I can only imagine the riot act that was read in the Kilkenny changing room at half-time because they scored the first five points of the second-half to go ahead. Seanie Quinn got us level, but with 10 minutes left they were three points ahead and must have thought they were well on their way to the semi-final.

But we weren't going to give up. Frankie Keenan doubled the ball into the net to equalise. With five minutes left, Aidan McNaughton stood over a '65' and pinged it straight over the bar. Now it was time to hold on… but Kilkenny got themselves one last chance from a '65' of their own.

Michael Walsh was the man taking it.

He hit it wide. That was it, we had won. But then the referee looked over at his linesman and saw he had his flag up. Something was wrong.

The referee jogged over to his linesman and they had a chat. Whether one of our players was standing too close to Walsh, when he was hitting the '65' or something else had happened, the up-shot was that the referee told Walsh he could hit it again. The worst thing was, the linesman was a Loughgiel man... Gerard McCloskey.

I couldn't believe it. I shouted over to him:

'WHAT THE HELL ARE YOU DOING, GERARD?'

It didn't matter. Walsh was getting another chance. This time he dropped it short and they got another shot off, but this one was definitely wide.

We'd beaten Kilkenny in Nowlan Park!

After the Leinster final the year before, the Kilkenny mentors had told us how it would be great for hurling if we could beat them one day and they'd be the first to congratulate us.

They didn't darken the door of our changing-room after our win.

AFTER A TREK to Rathdowney, then another one to Kilkenny, it was time to head down the country again for the semi-final against Wexford in Wexford Park. Those minor teams probably hold the record for the most miles travelled in a championship, and on the way down to matches our corner-forward Shane Caldwell had a wee ritual.

We'd always stop at Donnelly's filling station between Newry and Dundalk, the last filling station before you crossed the border. We were young fellas and we'd be in the shop buying all our junk food... the crisps and sweets we'd need to keep us going on the long journey down south. And Shane always bought a sticker of an Antrim crest... and stuck it on the back window of the mini-bus.

For some reason, when we were travelling down to Wexford. the filling station wasn't open that day, so we had to wait to get all our junk food – but Shane never got his Antrim sticker for the back window. I don't know how many of the other boys thought about that, but it always stuck in my head.

My dad was very superstitious. He never would have walked under a ladder, and he didn't like magpies. He wouldn't have driven on a Friday the 13th. I think I got that off him.

A couple of years later, in 1982, we'd won the county championship and the Ulster title. I managed to break a mirror in my bedroom and, after hearing the noise, my mum came in.

'For God's sake, don't tell your da!'

We still had an All-Ireland to go for, and a broken mirror in the house of the manager and the captain wouldn't have gone down well at all. So, I never told him. I don't know if that did the trick because we ended up winning the All-Ireland.

Although we wouldn't win another county championship until 1989! Seven years later.

WE WERE ABOUT to be back in the Leinster final for the second year in-a-row. With a bit over 10 minutes left of our semi-final against Wexford we were five points ahead and had just been given a penalty. We'd dominated them for the whole match and should have been even further ahead, but had a goal disallowed when the referee over-ruled one of his umpires who had waved the green flag.

After the match, I was talking to the Wexford man who ran the wee tuck shop, whose door was right in line with that goal, and asked him what his view of it was?

'Was it over the line?'

'By at least a foot!'

But we were still five points up with a penalty to come. Aidan McNaughton hit the target but they managed to stop it, and get it cleared. With five minutes left the Wexford corner-forward got a ball and headed straight for me. I don't know how many steps he took before he ran into me… but it was a lot.

The whistle went, but it wasn't for a free out.

One scored penalty later, and they were level. I think that knocked the stuffing out of us. They got two more points and it was them in the Leinster final instead of us.

We sat in the dressing-room for about an hour after that match, just shell-shocked. I cried my eyes out that day. I'm sure I wasn't the only one. We knew a big chance had gotten away from us; we thought we had been robbed because of some of the refereeing decisions and we just generally felt sorry for ourselves.

I can't remember the Wexford mentors coming in to talk to us – I'm sure they did. I do remember Hugh McPoland, who was county chairman, and who I don't remember seeing at any match before that, coming in and telling us we were a credit to the county and all that sort of stuff. I looked up at him and, thankfully, was able to bite my tongue. Saying what I wanted to say in that moment probably wouldn't have done me any good.

A lot of us went on to play for the county seniors and even though only myself, 'Sambo' and Donal Armstrong from the panel that went down to Wexford would be playing in 1989, when the seniors were chasing an All-Ireland, other players from that team were part of the foundations as Antrim started building through the 80s. But we didn't know that at the time.

We were all teenagers, so it's no surprise that defeat hit us hard. All of us felt there was an All-Ireland in that team, and when you're that age you don't know what's around the corner.

After beating us, Wexford beat Dublin in the Leinster final, but I never knew if they went on to win the All-Ireland. Or maybe I did know and just blocked it out. Either way, I was talking to Edmund Rowsome from Wexford years later and I asked him how Wexford got on after they beat us. They beat Galway after a replay in the semi-final, Edmund told me, and then they played Tipp in the All-Ireland final.

'Did they win?'

'No... and do you know who did the damage against us? Nicky English.'

Maybe losing to Wexford that day wasn't the worst thing that could have happened to me after all.

EVEN WITH THAT disappointment, playing on those minor teams was a brilliant experience. It created friends for life and, for a lot of us north Antrim boys, let us see a different world, not just around the country, but in our own county.

I was a young lad and when you went up to Belfast to play a match you thought you were going up to play a team full of boys with two heads. It was the height of The Troubles and you were going up to a city you were seeing every night on TV, with bombs going off and people being killed. Although aspects of The Troubles affected everybody in the north, no matter where you were, to an extent we were in our own wee bubble.

We were hardly out of whatever village we were from and the only time you did leave was to go to another wee north Antrim village to play a match. Going up to play these Belfast clubs, you may as well have given them a six-point lead.

But when I started playing underage county hurling, I got to know these guys and realise that when it came to all sorts of things, especially hurling, they were just the same as me. I think that's when we started to get the upper-hand on those

Belfast teams. In the younger age groups, we found it difficult to come out of the city with a result, but when we had boys on county teams with these Belfast ones, we started to get the results. We looked on them in a different way… as equals.

We also looked on them as friends, and it was great for us to be able to mix with boys from somewhere so different to where we were used to.

The team that reached the Leinster final had a lot of Loughgiel and Rossa boys, who had played against each other in the county minor final that year, and who are still great friends. When we were away with the county, I roomed with Seanie Quinn and we became good friends. In that final, Seanie came through and only had me to beat. I had always thought that if I was in a championship final, I would stop a fella no matter what I had to do. *If I have to take him out, I'll take him out and make sure he doesn't get back up.* But I didn't want to do that with Seanie coming through.

I still brought him down – they got a penalty and scored it – but I probably could have taken him out of the game without being sent off. But I didn't have the heart to do it, and I don't think that's a bad thing.

I've lost count of the number of great days and great laughs I've had with another Rossa man from that minor team, Ger Rogan – 'Rogie' – as we played together through the years for Antrim, and in the years since.

I got to know 'Sambo' McNaughton from playing on those minor teams and we stayed firm friends as we played together for the seniors over the next decade and more, and as we played against each other with Loughgiel and Cushendall. In 1980, my first full year of playing for the Loughgiel seniors, I was named North Antrim Hurler of the Year – a really big honour, and one I wasn't expecting at all. I was about 18 when I got it, and I remember reading in the paper – which was how I found out I won it – that I was the youngest ever. To tell the truth, I was a bit embarrassed by it.

But my record only lasted a year. The following season, when he was 17, 'Sambo' was named the North Antrim Hurler of the Year. So, we were great rivals… but great friends.

We were playing them in a championship match in Dunloy and he stepped up to the ball to hit a penalty…

'Come on now, Sambo. Hit me right here… drive it at the whites of my eyes!'

He threw up the ball and nearly missed it he was laughing so much. After that penalty, he came up to me, still laughing.

That's the way we were.

When Antrim were playing Offaly in the 1985 All-Ireland semi-final at the Athletic Grounds in Armagh, we were over in the social club killing time before the game. There was a pool table and Sambo says:

'Right, game of pool, first frame is for the Feis Cup.'

I beat him – and Loughgiel had already won the Feis Cup that year. 'Sambo' wasn't finished.

'Right, this time we're playing for the championship!'

He won – and the next month Cushendall beat us in the championship final. Every year after that he would challenge me to a game of pool… 'for the championship'. I was superstitious enough to turn him down every time, just in case.

Those teams gave me some great friends who have stood by me to this day.

PART **TWO**

'That's you boys... away yous go!'

Niall and his teammates on the Antrim team that shocked Kilkenny in Nowlan Park in the 1980 Leinster Championship.

Niall accepts the cup (left) after Loughgiel's historic victory over Ballycastle in the 1982 Antrim Senior Championship final, and shakes hands with his friend and county teammate 'Sambo' McNaughton before going into battle against one another.

The Loughgiel squad who were All-Ireland champions in 1983.

« CHAPTER 3 »

LIVING UNDER THE same roof as one of the county senior hurling selectors didn't give me any inside track on finding out if I was going to make it onto the panel.

It wasn't a case of my father telling me across the dinner table that I'd been picked. Like every season, the county put out the call for clubs to send any players they thought were county standard to trials. It was 1979, I was 17 with another year to come in the minors, and my name made it onto the list Loughgiel sent to the county.

So I went to the trials, did my best and was invited onto the panel. I can't remember how I found out, but I know it wasn't from my dad. He never mentioned it – that's just the way he was. He never wanted to show any favouritism. There was a new goalkeeper at training, and it just so happened to be his son.

I do remember crying when I found out – I was so proud.

That's something that never left me – the pride in being given an Antrim jersey and asked to represent my county. It's something I never took for granted and was one of the reasons I stopped playing for the county when I did. I wasn't going to go through the motions or take up a spot I didn't deserve, if I didn't think I was good enough. Playing for your county is too big an honour to treat it like that.

As soon as I started with the county, I knew things were on a different level. Training was different, fitness levels were different, everything was a bit quicker.

Everyone there was the best in the county, so that was the level you had to be at.

And then when you went to play against other county teams, that was a step up again. You were fit to see the boys you saw on TV at close range. Like that day seeing Jimmy Keaveney at Croke Park – but this time it was the hurling heroes I'd grown up in awe of.

That took a bit of getting used to. It's something I never really got used to.

MY VIEW OF all those players in my first year was from the bench.

Jim Corr was first choice goalkeeper, and a good one. We were different types of goalkeeper. Jim was probably a bit flashy for my liking, but that was his style and it served him well. He was a replacement All Star in 1976 – a big honour, especially for a county like Antrim.

I obviously wanted to be out playing, but was nowhere near Jim's class and I learned a hell of a lot sitting on the bench. You'll always learn more out on the pitch, but while I was a sub, I wasn't sitting talking to whoever was beside me. I was glued to the match. Sometimes I would watch the other goalkeepers... how they operated, what way they moved, where they put their puckouts.

Sometimes, I watched their half-back line... who put their hand up, who didn't. But I was mostly watching the opposition forward line, especially the inside forwards. *Which way do they like to turn? What angle are they running at the goals at? Which side are they striking on? What way are they hand-passing the ball?* Back then, you could hand-pass the ball into the net and you could have an idea of where the ball was going when a player threw it up to do a 'traditional' hand-pass, across their body.

But the nightmare was when forwards started to throw up the ball and used their hand like they were batting it into the net. When they did that, you had no idea where it was going. Tony Doran put three past me one day like that down at Wexford Park.

I HAD PLENTY of time to study other teams from the bench, as that's where I spent my entire first year with the county team. Gilly McIlhatton was the manager when I came onto the panel, but it was a team effort with my dad, Con Grego, Jim Nelson and other members of the hurling board all involved in one way or another, as they always were.

If you want to talk about legends of Antrim hurling, you have to talk about Gilly McIlhatton. Gilly's from the Mitchel's club in west Belfast and was involved with all sorts of Antrim teams through the years and on every hurling board and committee going. He was manager when Antrim won the All-Ireland 'B' championship in 1978 and would go on win two more in 1980 and '81. More than 20 years later, he was manager when Antrim won the junior All-Ireland in 2002. He's just a great hurling man, and when you were playing for Gilly, he instilled total belief in you.

It was that Belfast thing again. Gilly didn't care who we were playing – set them down in front of us and we'll take them on. A real wee warrior, a wee winner. Any time you saw him, there was a smile on his face and that spread throughout the team, just the joy of being there with your county. And Gilly had the loudest laugh you've ever heard.

I used to go up to his house with my dad and listen to them tell stories about old hurlers and when they used to play. It was a pleasure to sit quietly in the corner and hear all this hurling knowledge being shared.

Gilly wouldn't have been into tactics as much as my dad would have been, but he knew what you were capable of and what he could get out of you. Though he didn't always get it right.

We were playing Cork in an All-Ireland under-21 semi-final and Gilly had told the defenders... and me before the match...

'This Tony O'Sullivan fella, keep pushing him to his left... he's got no left side!'

The first two digs he hit at me on his left side were past me before I knew it, and he hit the crossbar with another one. I wasn't looking forward to see what he could do off his right side.

Con Grego was another Belfast man who, if you were feeling down or had a bad game, would be the first to lift you. Con was loud and bubbly – there's no way you'd feel nervous going into games as Con was in your face and getting you going.

I got to know these men long before I was on the county team. Any match that was up in Loughgiel, the hurling board officials would call into our house on the way back home; my mum would have tea for them and they'd sit and talk hurling for hours.

EVEN THOUGH I was joining a panel full of players I played against every week at club level, I was still starry-eyed. I think it was natural with me being so young. It was hard not to look up to the players in that side who had been around for years.

It was a little intimidating to be in a changing room with the county players. It's not that I didn't feel part of the set-up, but I couldn't rub shoulders with the older boys who were there so long. It wasn't my place. I hung around with Brian Donnelly and Aidan McNaughton, the younger lads who I had played with underage. I thought you had to earn your spurs and get to the level of the established players.

The fact my dad was part of the management team probably meant I had to work a bit harder to earn my spurs. If Gilly had had his way, I would have made my debut a little earlier than I did. My dad was the one who said I wasn't ready.

He was never going to show favouritism, and probably went out of his way to do the opposite. I had to prove to him that I was even a *wee bit better* than I was, before he would play me. It was the same with the club and same for cousins who would have played for Loughgiel. You had to be that wee bit better before he would play you, so there was no doubt you had earned your place.

I only found out after I finished playing that the reason he held me back with the county is that he didn't want me to go in so young, make a fool of myself and, perhaps, then I wouldn't be fit to play again. I was only 17 when I started and he wanted me to be ready so that when the chance came, I would be fit to take it with both hands and not let go of it.

He was right but, like so many things, at the time I didn't see that. I was sub goalkeeper and I wasn't being used and I thought… *What's the point in me being here and training, if I'm never going to get a chance?*

Once I did get my chance, I honestly thought that I would be there until I decided to walk away. I wasn't being big-headed; I just think any goalkeeper needs to believe in their ability and be confident – but you can't go overboard.

I remember Frank Ward saying to me that my problem was actually that I wasn't cocky enough, maybe thinking that I needed to push myself forward more. But in my mind, I could never let myself get cocky because a goalkeeper who comes across as too confident is leaving himself wide open. You are going to make mistakes, no matter what. Nobody's perfect and when a goalkeeper makes a mistake, it's magnified, and if you are cocky you'll soon hear about it. I tried to believe in my own ability without shouting about it. I made plenty of mistakes and I hold my hands up to them, but I like to think no one could ever say I made them because I was a cocky so-and-so.

Frank was a super hurler, he's is a super man, and he taught me a lot when I came onto the county team. Frank was a seasoned player and he took me under his wing. It also helped that he was a corner-back who would put his head in anywhere to save you.

I went to school with Frank's wife, and back then when we travelled to training and matches in cars, me and my dad would leave Frank home, but he wouldn't let us go and we'd not get back to Loughgiel until all hours.

I CAME IN at a good time.

Things were starting to build. The belief wasn't really there yet through the whole team that we were capable of doing this or doing that, but I always believed in the players we had. I didn't care who we were playing, I knew if we went out and hit a good day, we could put it up to *them* and maybe beat *them*. My feeling was that if we played Cork today and they beat us by 30 points, if we had to play them again next week, I wouldn't be scared of them.

That's just how I was; I was confident in my teammates because I knew they were good hurlers. That feeling only grew the longer I was there and the more players came into the team, like 'Sambo', 'Beaver', 'Cloot' and Ciaran Barr.

And the team I came into was full of great hurlers in the first place. The Ballycastle team of the early-80s was the best I played against at club level and they were the backbone of that Antrim side. You had Terence Barton, Peter Boyle, Stephen Boyle, Paul Smith, the Donnellys... sometimes six of them on the same county team. It still mystifies me that Danny McNaughton never won an All Star.

Brian Donnelly was only on the team a year longer than I was, but he had the same attitude as me... that Antrim could go out and compete against *anybody*. When the RTE cameras came up before the 1989 All-Ireland final, Mick Dunne asked Brian, 'Do you see yourself with a realistic chance?'

Brian couldn't believe the question.

'Since I've been hurling at underage level I've yet to go into a match thinking I'm not going to win!'

After hurling against Brian from underage level it was no surprise to me that he thought like that. That sort of belief was infectious. Gerard Cunningham – 'Cut' – was someone I looked up to when I started hurling for the county because he didn't care one bit who he was marking. It was more Belfast confidence.

We were playing Tipperary in the league in 1984 and Nicky English had just won his first All Star. 'Cut' was at my dad at half-time… 'Let me mark English, Neil'.

He was mad to get at him. Maybe some of us boys in north Antrim would have gone into our shell… *Oh no, I'm marking Nicky English, I'm not good enough for that.*

Maybe just a wee bit too respectful. I know I would have been like that if I had to mark someone. But the Belfast boys had a different attitude and that's an attitude you need in a side.

There was one day when 'Cut' maybe bit off more than he could chew. We played Dublin in a league match in Croke Park as the curtain-raiser for a Compromise Rules match between Ireland and Australia. Back then, the Ireland-Australia matches were full-scale brawls with the occasional bit of football breaking out.

We were coming off the pitch and the Aussie boys were standing there pumped up and growling, muscles bulging, sweat lashing off them.

'Let's get into these Irish scum,' that sort of thing… and wee 'Cut' told them what he thought of that sort of talk in Croke Park, and sort of brandished his stick at them. They hunted us back into the dressing-room and were battering at the door to get at us.

They weren't one bit worried that we were the ones carrying the sticks.

AFTER A YEAR of sitting on the bench, I thought my chance had finally come in the first match of the league in October 1980. We were playing Kerry in Loughgiel and Jim, who was based down in Shannon, couldn't make it. But when the team was announced I was still a substitute. There were two goalkeepers on the panel and I thought, with one of them away, the jersey would go to the other one… me.

Instead, my dad and Gilly took Randal McDonnell not just out of corner-forward, but out of retirement and put him in goals. I was so disappointed, but I never questioned it. It was my dad who brought it up when we got home from training the night to team was announced.

'I suppose you're disappointed not playing?'

'Well, I'm sub goalkeeper and I thought whenever the regular goalkeeper wasn't there I'd be in.'

'You're not ready yet!'

I still wasn't convinced.

'I don't think you're ready for this step just yet, you're still learning. Randal McDonnell kept goals for Ulster when he was a minor and he's the right man for Sunday.'

When Sunday came round, Randal pulled off a save in the last minute that I'd never have gotten near and Antrim beat Kerry. That was a lesson learned for me.

For the rest of the league, Gilly had to keep pushing my dad to play me and when the very last game came around my dad obviously thought I was ready. It just so happened to be against Kilkenny in Nowlan Park.

When I was told I was playing, I was up to high doh. It wasn't that I was panicking about playing Kilkenny, it was just pure excitement. I couldn't wait. 'Woody' made his debut that day too and, although we lost, I had a good game and I did enough to convince my dad that I was ready.

JUST LIKE THE Intermediate Championship was the big goal for Antrim in 1970, in 1980 it was the 'B' championship, that had replaced it in 1974. My dad was manager when Antrim lost the first final in 1974 to Kildare. Kildare went on to play Galway in the All-Ireland quarter-final, and that was the big carrot for teams. Antrim eventually managed to win it in 1978 and put up a decent show against Galway. There was another carrot for teams in the 'B' championship – if you won it two years out of three, you'd be promoted to the All-Ireland Championship proper.

In 1979, Antrim missed their chance when they lost to Kildare in the semi-final, and after losing to them in the semi again the following year it was back to the drawing board in 1981. The league hadn't gone very well. That win over Kerry – that Randal McDonnell save – had kept us up. It was the only match we won.

Still, heading into the 'B' championship we were the top ranked team. Kerry were the only team we could play who were in the same division as us in the league. Everyone else in the competition were teams we should fancy ourselves against. But that hadn't stopped us from losing to teams like that in the past, so we were on our guard.

I kept my place after the Kilkenny match, so when the championship came around, I was the first name on the team-sheet and was determined I'd stay there. We went down to Keady in the first round to play Armagh in a match we were expected to win with a lot to spare – and we did. Dessie Donnelly got a hat-trick – not for the first time – and that put us into a semi-final against Kildare, who as well as knocking us out the past two years were the reigning champions.

They started like they were going to knock us out again... we only scored a point in the first 25 minutes against the breeze in Croke Park. But we managed to get back into the match by half-time, and were only three behind with the wind at our backs in the second-half.

Two goals from Dessie in the first 10 minutes after the break sent us on our way and the defence really knuckled down to keep Kildare out, as we won fairly comfortably in the end.

After the previous two years, beating Kildare, especially in the semi-final, got a real monkey off our back. Eight months after I sat on the bench watching Randal McDonnell help us beat Kerry in our first match in the league, I had the goalkeeper's jersey for an All-Ireland final against Kerry at Croke Park.

The match itself was completely forgettable.

It took 20 minutes for anyone to score and it was only three points each at half-time. I had very little to do, but at the other end we were hitting a lot of wides, and we only managed three points in the second-half as well. Thankfully, Brian Donnelly got a goal and Kerry needed an equaliser to force a replay.

We were like a different team the next week in Parnell Park. Eddie and Brian Donnelly got a couple of early goals and we were cruising at half-time, eight points up. The Donnellys scored another goal each in the second-half and we ran away with it.

Kerry got a goal too, the first one I had conceded in the championship, although my clean-sheets weren't really anything to do with me. Our defence was great – Frank Ward, Sean McNaughton and Kevin and 'Hippy' Donnelly were all really good defenders and they showed it that day.

There was only one man to blame for the Kerry goal and he was my own man. A ball was coming in and Gerard Cunningham pulled on it in the air, but missed it, and swung back and broke his stick clean across my knee. I had caught the ball but dropped it when 'Cut' caught me and they scored a goal from it.

Later that season, we were playing St John's up in Loughgiel. We were two points up and they got a '65' going into the last few minutes. 'Cut' came up from half-back and stood beside me. He turned to me and grinned.

'Which knee is it again?'

He wasn't joking.

After winning the 'Home' final we had the real final to play, and London came to Loughgiel for it. London didn't play in the league back then so it was nearly impossible to tell just how strong they'd be. They played the winners of the 'Home' final every year for the 'B' championship, and some years they were better than others. They had put it up to Antrim in the 1978 final, but we had no idea how good they'd be when they got to Loughgiel three years later. They turned out to be pretty good.

They scored a couple of goals in the first-half and we were level at half-time. We tightened up a bit in the second-half but could never really pull away – a couple of goals from John Crossey and Brendan Laverty helped us hold them off and win our All-Ireland title.

That was our big goal for the season ticked-off and it put us into an All-Ireland quarter-final in Croke Park against Galway, who had made their breakthrough the previous year, winning their first All-Ireland in decades. They were obviously determined not to let go of it because they never let up against us. We got 3-11 – a good enough total – but Galway were relentless... they scored 6-23.

And they kept going for goals! I'm not sure I've faced so many shots in a match in my life. Six went past me, but I think I stopped about 20!

I came off at half-time convinced I was going to be taken off. Galway had already scored five goals. The fifth one was a nightmare. Joe Connolly came through and drove in a shot. I did the hard part by stopping it, but as he kept coming in, I tried to flick it over him and he blocked it into the net. As soon as that went in, I thought... *Jesus, that's me away now.* I walked off with my head down, sat down in the dressing-room and got ready to be told I wouldn't be coming out for the second-half. Someone sat down beside me. I think it was Gilly – it definitely wasn't my dad anyway.

'Right,' he said, 'you're going really well here, keep it going in the second-half.'

I had a cup of tea in my hand and had to set it down and look at him. I wasn't sure what match he was watching. But I went back out and managed to keep a clean-sheet as Galway kept firing in the shots on goal. It was only in the last couple of minutes that they got their sixth. We lost by 21 points but a couple of the papers gave me Man of the Match.

That night, my dad said to me, 'I suppose you think you did well?'

I knew I had had a good game and I told him I thought I did alright. He told me I'd never be a goalkeeper until I can come off against a Galway, a Cork or a Kilkenny... after only letting in one... or none!

'Then you're a goalkeeper!'

That became my yardstick, trying to get that six down to five, down to four... down to none. That's what kept me going every match I played after that.

I wasn't the only Antrim player who got some praise in the papers after the Galway match. Three points from our 3-11 came from sideline cuts that Mick O'Connell had sailed over the bar.

Mick was an established man in the Antrim midfield when I came into the team and I already knew what he could do from playing with him with Loughgiel since I came into the senior team. I was still playing with the juniors – which was basically the reserves – and on the verge of moving up to the first team when I was over on Rathlin Island to play a nurses' dance with Frankie McBride, Ciaran McHugh and Alistair McQuilkin. I had never been on Rathlin – the small island just across from Ballycastle – so we went for a drive to have a look around.

It was then I saw a boy in the middle of a field, all by himself with a hurling stick, hitting the ball up into the air and catching it, then dropping the ball and lifting it... going off on solo runs, stopping and turning... hitting the ball back into the air. Again, and again. I said to whoever was driving:

'Pull over, I want to see who the hell this is!'

It was Mick O'Connell. Mick had been over in Rathlin working and he was training for whatever match he had coming up the following Sunday. He didn't want to miss out, so was training away on his own, staying sharp. That was Mick O'Connell.

AFTER WE WON the All-Ireland, Gilly stepped down as manager and his replacement was a surprise. Kevin Donnelly was still on the panel and was the first choice full-back that season until he got injured before the B final against London.

But he was nominated for the manager's job and beat Jim Nelson to it, though it continued to be a team effort with Kevin inviting Jim on board. And other members of the hurling committee, like my dad, Con Grego, Gilly and Gerry McClory, who was the minor manager for our Leinster campaigns, were still involved.

The league was a difficult one and we only managed to win one match, down in Kerry, but we didn't play badly and put up decent shows at home against Kilkenny, who beat us by six points, and Limerick, who beat us by two.

They reorganised the league that season, which meant we weren't relegated, so we could turn our attention to defending our 'B' championship title, and if we managed that, we would move up to the All-Ireland Championship proper. After missing out in 1979 and '80 we were determined to make this one count.

After the league finished at the end of February, Kevin stood down because of family commitments and my dad had stepped in ahead of the championship, keeping the likes of Gilly, Con Grego and Jim Nelson on board. We had exactly the same job ahead of us as we did the year before.

Like the year before, we played Armagh in the first round and we hammered them again. Dessie Donnelly tortured the Armagh defence *again* and scored 5-4, but we knew the semi-final – the fourth year in-a-row we were playing Kildare at that stage – would be a completely different story.

For most of the match it looked like Kildare would beat us for the third year out of four. They were a point up at half-time and we didn't lead in the second-half until about five minutes left when Danny McNaughton scored. Danny scored a couple more points and we were into a 'Home' final against Carlow.

That went much more smoothly than the Kildare match and by half-time we already knew things would have to go badly wrong if we were going to lose. Brian Donnelly scored a couple of goals in the space of about five minutes, Danny McNaughton kept knocking over points and, in the end, we won by 11 points.

After London came to Loughgiel for the previous year's final, this time we would have to travel over to England, knowing a win would mean we'd qualify for the All-Ireland Championship proper.

Our hotel in London wasn't like anywhere any of us had been in in our lives. The hurlers always felt like poor relations compared to the footballers, and I'm not sure who booked it, but that weekend we were living the high life.

There was a mini-bar in every room. So, we were told... 'Right, don't be touching anything because it'll be put down next to your room bill and will have to be paid for!'

So that was fair enough, but in the afternoon my dad and Gilly ordered some tea and sandwiches. Gilly got up to pay for it and my dad said, 'Never worry, I'll get it'.

'That'll be £27, please.'

In 1982, £27 would have bought you every cup of tea and sandwich in Loughgiel and Cloughmills, with plenty of change to head over to Dunloy with.

It looked like the match at Ruislip would be as easy as the one against Carlow, when Dessie Donnelly scored a goal in the first minute even though we were playing into a strong breeze. We kept playing well and the only reason they were within three points at half-time was that they scored a penalty just before the break.

Dessie scored another goal early in the second-half but we could never pull away and when they scored a goal near the end, there were just two points in it. We managed to hang on, but it took a great tackle from 'Hippy' to stop them scoring what would have been a winning goal. It was only his first last-gasp intervention of the day.

After the match, we were heading to airport on our way home and 'Hippy' bent down to his bag. You could hear the clinks before the zip was opened, so we knew what was coming. A few rooms' worth of mini-bars were in there with his gear, and the boys got stuck into it before we reached the airport, celebrating the fact Antrim were back in the All-Ireland Senior Championship proper for the first time in years.

Before that, we had our last All-Ireland quarter-final to play as the B champions. Galway were waiting for us again and the match in Croke Park followed the same script to the one from the year before.

We scored a point more this time in another decent total of 3-12, but Galway were just as ruthless, scoring six goals again… as well as 19 points, although the same day Galway beat us by 16 points, Cork beat Waterford in the Munster final by more than 30 points. We'd gotten out of the 'B' championship and more players were starting to come through.

'Sambo' and Ger Rogan had started their first championship matches against Carlow and it might not have looked it, but we did honestly feel we were getting closer.

THE MATCHES WE played in Division Two or Division 1B – it didn't matter what you called it – could be tough, *tough* battles. We were one of a group of teams along with Kerry, Westmeath, Dublin and Kildare, who seemed to be playing against each other every year. We all got to know each other really well – who the best players were, how they played, who you had to keep a close eye on. It was nearly like club games; we played so often, and games could get nearly as intense.

We had a lot of battles with Kerry, in the league and the 'B' championship. They had a big full-forward and we had had a run-in in Croke Park in the 1981 'B' championship Home final. Actually, it was more than a run-in – he battered me black and blue all day.

Later that year, we were playing them in the league, down in Ardfert, and you always knew you'd get it tight down there. At that time, I had lost some weight, got my place in the team and was keeping it off. I was in good shape, sharp on my feet – maybe the best shape I was ever in.

I was quick off my line and was able to be out first to just about every ball that came my way, and every time I did and came out by him to clear, he'd block me across the wrists. *Every single time.*

I was getting more and more frustrated and then I got a ball, was coming out to clear it and as I side-stepped him, he hit me with the heel of the stick across the back as I drove the ball up the field. I turned.

'The next time you hit me… I'm going to drop you!'

I'd had enough – but my dad always said to me, 'If I ever see you hitting a boy on a hurling field, I'll come on and take you out myself'.

So, *how was I going to do this?* The one thing I knew was, he wasn't going to get another warning. So, I came out with the ball again and the same thing happened. He nailed me on the wrist.

I hit the ball up the field and this time, on my way back, I dropped him. Straightaway, I heard the whistle going. Noel O'Donoghue from Dublin was the referee and I could see him running down the field… straight for me.

That's it, I thought, *I'm away.*

'RIGHT,' said Noel… 'NAMES!'

We gave him our names and I was expecting him to point to the line – about where my dad was standing.

'Right. I'm watching the pair of you… no more of that!'

We went in at half-time and my dad said to me, 'What are you playing at?'

I told him your man was beating me black and blue. So, he took me to the side and said, 'If you want to take him out, this is how you do it'.

I couldn't believe it.

We were 10 minutes into the second-half and nothing had changed. I caught a big high ball coming in and could see him heading for me. But now I had a plan. I put the ball on the stick and soloed out, straight at him. I threw the ball up, turned the heel of the stick and pulled about six inches above the ball.

My dad told me he dropped like a bag of spuds. He was taken off and that was it.

And we won the match handy as well.

We played them again in the league a couple of years later on an awful snowy day. Tommy Murray was a great Antrim supporter from Ardoyne in Belfast, but was living down in Tipperary and he went to all our matches. Tommy and his son Fergal were maybe the only Antrim supporters in Nowlan Park when we beat Kilkenny in that minor match in 1980. That day against Kerry, Tommy was standing behind my goals.

The match was another battle as usual and a row started near the goals, and spilled off the pitch right up against the wire. I wasn't involved in it this time – at least I don't think so. But the big Kerry man was in the middle of it and Tommy reached over the wire with an umbrella and hit him over the head with it. So, your man reached over and grabbed Tommy by the tie… Tommy always wore a suit and tie, always a well-dressed man. But the tie was clip-on and Tommy stepped back and nailed him again.

Fair play to you, Tommy! I thought. *You got in your slap and the ref can't do anything about it.* Tommy used to come up to my dad with a bottle of poitín from Tipperary. He landed a up at the shop after my dad had died.

'Where's the auld boy?'

'Tommy, he's lying up there in that graveyard,' I told him.

Tommy didn't know what to say, he was devastated.

MY DAD WAS made the permanent manager for the 1982-'83 season, and he had the usual suspects there with him still… like Gilly, Jim Nelson, Con Grego and Gerry McClory all still on board.

Because Loughgiel were going for the Ulster title and then the All-Ireland, I ended up only playing a couple of matches in the league, with Jim Nelson's son Hugh in goals for the rest of them.

It was a decent league for Antrim, but the top two teams in Division Two – Laois and Limerick – were way ahead of the rest, so we never challenged for promotion. We didn't have to play in the 'B' championship but we didn't go straight into the All-Ireland quarter-final. First, we had to play against a team we knew all too well. Kerry won the 'B' championship which meant they'd be playing us in a preliminary round match, with the winners going on to play Galway in the quarter-final.

We played them down in Crumlin, in Dublin, on a boiling hot July day. As usual, it was a battle, and this time blood was drawn. Dessie Donnelly was bitten on the arm, and it must have been because of how hot it was, but he just wouldn't stop bleeding. No matter how many layers of plasters and bandages they put on him, it didn't seem like the blood would ever stop pumping out of his arm.

Thankfully, it did eventually, though it didn't slow him down, at least not until we got back to the hotel that night where I had to cut Dessie's steak for him because he couldn't use his left arm.

We had the match won by half-time. Kerry only scored a couple of points and our forwards – Dessie included – were doing serious damage. Dessie and Brian Donnelly scored two of our goals and 'Beaver' McCarry, who was making his championship debut, got the other one. The team was coming together.

Another quarter-final against Galway brought another big defeat – 20 points this time – but that match in Mullingar was maybe the best game I had in my whole career.

PJ Molloy came through and hit one that I went full stretch to stop. The ball bounced out and Noel Lane doubled on it. I was lying on my back but got up and stopped it, and then Molloy came in again and I stopped that one… and put it out for a '65'. I made another couple of point-blank saves from Joe Connolly and, in the end, kept Galway to three goals.

Joe would have been friendly with my dad and myself – Loughgiel used to go down to Castlegar to play in tournaments and we stayed with him – and in the second-half he came through with the ball and went to hand-pass it and I dove across to stop the ball. But when I looked there was no ball there.

He still had it in his hand and then just put it into the net with me on my back. I felt so stupid that I'd bought his dummy, and dived at nothing. Joe patted me on the back and laughed.

'It was the only way I was going to beat you.'

I was happy with how I'd played, but obviously disappointed that we had lost. Though the biggest disappointment was that I hadn't been captain that season.

At that time, the county champions provided the county captain. We won the championship and the first game of the league was one of the two I actually played that year. It was against Wicklow in Loughgiel and when the team was read out... the captain was Brian Gormley from Rossa.

I thought it would have been me because I was captain of the county champions. I never said anything but later on my dad sat me down. 'I suppose you thought you should have been captaining the team?'

'Yeah, I did. Or at least somebody from Loughgiel... Mick O'Connell or someone else.'

'Do you not think Brian Gormley is more worthy to captain the team than you are?'

'He is!' I said, and I did believe that. Brian had given so many years of service and I had only been there for a couple of years, but I was still surprised.

My dad obviously didn't think it was the right time for me to be the county captain, and he decided to change the rules about it. As usual, he was probably right – I was playing very well and he maybe thought the captaincy would be a distraction – but that didn't stop it being disappointing.

In hindsight it's even more disappointing, as I never got the chance again.

ANOTHER CHANGE TO the championship format meant big things for us the next season. Congress had passed a motion to put Antrim or Galway straight into the All-Ireland semi-final in alternate years. Every other year, we'd have to play the winners of the 'B' championship but, in the first season under the new rules, in 1984, we'd be playing the Munster champions for the right to reach the All-Ireland final.

We were still in Division Two and I missed the first couple of matches of the league because I was so busy with the music at the time. Seamus Richmond had retired and I had taken over the running of the band and doing the bookings. Paul Smith, the sub goalkeeper from Ballycastle, came in for those first two matches and, as it turned out, they were the only ones we won – against Wicklow and Kildare.

We played well in other matches and ran Dublin and Offaly close. Then, in the Centenary Cup in April against Waterford, we only lost by a point when they scored a last-minute goal... and the referee played a minute short in the second-half.

But that Waterford match was our last competitive game before the All-Ireland semi-final. So, while we waited and tried to get decent challenge matches where we could, Cork won the Centenary Cup before beating Limerick and Tipp to win Munster.

The result of the semi-final wasn't really a surprise to anyone and went along the same lines as our quarter-finals against Galway the previous three years. In the end Cork beat us by 24 points, but we managed to stay with them for nearly half an hour. Danny McNaughton got a goal from a rebound after Dessie Donnelly had a penalty saved and we were only two behind, but after Kevin Hennessy got Cork's first goal, they ran away from us.

When I had started with the county, we were trying to get out of the 'B' championship. Now we were going straight into an All-Ireland semi-final. So, we had made progress, but it was an opportunity that wouldn't be of any use unless we took it.

We needed to take another step forward to prove we belonged.

« CHAPTER 4 »

WHEN THE 1982 season started, you'd have done well to find anyone outside Loughgiel who thought we'd be challenging for the championship that year.

Ballycastle had been the dominant team in Antrim for years, winning three in-a-row and reaching the All-Ireland final in 1980. Then in 1981 Cushendall came along and beat them in the county final to win their first ever Senior Championship. Loughgiel hadn't been in the final since 1974, and the last county title in '71 felt like an age, given how that great team had dominated the decade before.

The team had been in transition and although a lot of us had won with underage sides and had made our way on to the seniors, there was no expectation we'd be putting it up to Ballycastle or Cushendall.

Or even that we'd beat St John's in the first round.

A few weeks into the 1982 season and anyone left in Loughgiel who thought we had a chance had probably disappeared too. At the start of May we played Glenariffe in the Feis Cup. They had been an intermediate team the year before and we weren't expected to have too many problems. We were terrible, and lost. My dad came into the changing room.

'Right boys, I'm not going to say anything now!' he began. 'We'll have a meeting on Tuesday and then we're going to talk about what we're going to do. I wouldn't watch that performance again.

'If you want to hurl, it's time to get the finger out. If you don't want to hurl, I'll pull this team out of the championship.'

There was a notice put in the parish bulletin in Loughgiel about an extraordinary meeting of the players and the management.

Just under a year later we were All-Ireland champions.

A BIG PART of the reason I won that North Antrim Hurler of the Year award when I was just into the Loughgiel senior team is that I had plenty of chances to make saves.

We were building a new team and it wasn't always an easy process.

When I was growing up, Johnny Coyle was the goalkeeper and the twin Lavertys – Liam and Sean – were the corner-backs. The twins had the reputation of being there to lay one on the corner-forwards but they were good hurlers.

Liam was the boy who would have kept me right when I started in the senior team and I don't think he got the credit he deserved for helping Loughgiel through that tough period of transition. We might have been in a match where we should have been getting beat by 25 points, but Liam being there meant it was only five or six.

My first ever Senior Championship match, in 1979, was actually my second championship match that day. I was on the senior panel and had played in the league, but was still able to play with our intermediate team because I hadn't played in the Senior Championship the previous year. The intermediate team had a championship match on a Sunday afternoon in Loughgiel, with the seniors set to play Armoy a couple of hours later.

So, after we had beaten Dwyer's in the intermediate match, I headed the 10 minutes up the road to Armoy to play for the seniors. We won both matches easily but that season ended – as they all seemed to do at that time – with Ballycastle beating us in the semi-final. We had a big half-time lead but, with the wind in the second-half, Ballycastle ran away from us.

After they beat us, they went on to become the first Antrim team to reach the All-Ireland club final, where they lost narrowly to Castlegar from Galway. Th thought that we'd be going one better than them at the end of the season was t' farthest thing from anybody's mind when the players and management sat dc for our meeting before the 1982 championship

THE FIRST ITEM on the agenda at that meeting was our discipline. We just gave away too many frees and we were told again that we would be pulled out of the championship unless we changed our attitude. The management sat us down.

'Yous boys all think yous are tough men!

'It takes a harder man to stand and get a knock with a hurling stick, set the ball down and walk on… than it does to hit a boy back with a stick!'

For the rest of that year our discipline was great. If you got hit, you set the ball down and walked away. If you gave away a free, there was no talking to the referee. He wasn't going to change his mind; he'd just move the ball forward and you'd hurt the team. We had three weeks until we were playing St John's in the championship and we worked on our discipline and our game-plan.

The management team that year was my dad, Liam McGarry, Dominic Casey and Danny McMullan, who was the coach and trainer and as good as I ever played under. Those Loughgiel teams of the 60s – all the teams through the club's history – was renowned for first-time hurling, and the players we had were suited to that. We wanted to just get that ball out of defence as quickly as possible and then it was up to the midfield to keep the ball moving.

The only boys with instructions to stop the ball were the two corner-forwards, to keep it from going wide. Then it was up to them to come out with the ball and lay it off to boys going through. That seemed to work for us and, thankfully, we had the players to make it work.

But things definitely didn't click right away. Against St John's in the first round we were nearly as bad as we were against Glenariffe. It wasn't until Brendan Laverty's goal in the second-half that we felt safe. We eventually won by four points and moved on to a quarter-final against Sarsfield's.

The scoreline was much better – we won by 14 points – but the performance was still way short of what it would take to win a championship. Joe McGurk – one of the famous family from Lavey, whose brother Johnny won a football All-Ireland with Derry in 1993 – was playing for us that year. Against Sarsfield's, he was about to be taken off… but said to my dad, 'Give me 10 minutes Neil'.

He scored a goal but he took a bad knock, and we went on to the win the championship but Joe didn't play in any more matches. Soon after that, Joe and Alec Connelly started to video our matches; Joe would commentate with Alec on the camera. There wasn't much video being done of club matches at that stage so we were able to sit down and watch the games, and see where we were going wrong and what we could do to improve.

We were in a county semi-final, but our two wins wouldn't have had anyone else quaking in their boots – especially not Cushendall, who were hot favourites after winning their first-ever Senior Championship the year before.

We played them in Dunloy and there was a gale blowing straight down the pitch. We played with the wind in the first-half and got up a good lead. We were 10 points ahead thanks to a couple of Brendan McGarry goals, and another one from Brendan Laverty. It wasn't just the wind, however. We were playing well and held Cushendall to just a point for nearly the whole half.

If we needed a reminder the match wasn't over, we got it when Cushendall scored three quick points before half-time.

Turning to face the wind, we knew we'd need to battle to hold on and then, three minutes into the second-half, 'Sambo' got a goal. From there until the end, we were holding on. We managed to keep out a penalty, but Cushendall kept knocking over the points and we couldn't make any headway against the breeze.

They had it back to within two, but 'Woody' scored a point with about five minutes left to give us *some* breathing space. Still, it nearly wasn't enough.

With the match on the blow and our lead back down to two, Dominic McKeegan was coming through with the ball and our full-back PJ O'Mullan came out to meet him. I can still see Alistair McGuile standing next to me... all on his own on the edge of the square.

One hand-pass and he would have taken that ball and buried it.

That would have been it. No Antrim, no Ulster... no All-Ireland. But our defenders ushered Dominic out and we held on.

We were in a county final, Loughgiel's first in nearly 10 years and the first most of us in the team – eight or nine of us were still under-21s – had ever been in. We had five weeks until we faced Ballycastle, and Danny McMullan didn't waste a second of those five weeks.

From a team that started the year as not great trainers, he had us hitting our absolute peak in those five weeks. He knew exactly how to get us to just the right point going into a big match. Danny was a genius as far as that went and whenever he spoke, you just sat down, shut up and let him do his thing.

In those five weeks, Danny had us flying. People who were at the final said afterwards that when we came out onto the pitch that day against Ballycastle they knew we were going to win. There was something about us and it was Danny McMullan who put *that* into us.

Ballycastle were the favourites, in their sixth final in-a-row and they just sauntered out of the changing room onto the pitch. We burst out onto the field and nearly went through half the Ballycastle team in front of us. We were mad to get at it.

When we ran out in Dunloy, we were ready.

And when we ran out, I was the man running out first.

EVERY YEAR, THE senior captain was picked at the AGM and that season Dominic Casey, who was going to be one of the selectors, proposed me. It got unanimous backing and I'd only just turned 20... but I was the Loughgiel senior captain.

I was chuffed to bits.

I went home that night and cried my eyes out; I was so proud – one of the proudest days of my life.

But as proud as I was, my job was really just taking the toss.

I barked out directions to my defence but that's nothing I wouldn't be doing anyway. We were lucky in that we had a man in every line of our team who was a leader, every one of them could be seen as a captain. Everyone kept each other going. There was never a word turned on each other the whole time.

If someone made a mistake, it was... 'Right, next ball'.

All I really had to do differently was go up and take the toss. As it happened, we won it for every game in the championship. I played with the wind every time. My father always taught me to take the advantage when it's there, because you never know when it's going the change.

So, I went up to take the toss with the referee Seamus O'Hare and Eddie Donnelly, who was captaining Ballycastle. We won it again. But taking the toss in the county final felt a bit different. I was that nervous I played the wrong way... and pointed straight into the wind.

I remember going back to the goals and saying to PJ McMullan, 'I won the toss and played the wrong road!'

'Forget it!' said PJ.

We just got buckled in and that was it.

PJ went on to be one of the selectors with Antrim when we reached the All-Ireland final in 1989, and was Loughgiel manager when we won the county title that year as well. When he played, he gave you great protection. PJ was a big strong man. One year, Castlegar came up to Loughgiel to stay and play a couple of matches. We had a big barn dance one of the nights they were up and, after it, a big ring was constructed and PJ and their full-back – one of the Connollys – were taking runs at each other like two goats butting… hitting each other with shoulders to see which one was the toughest.

Your man had to quit… PJ was the boy left standing.

Thankfully, playing the wrong way didn't hold us back and we tore into Ballycastle, but we needed to settle some nerves first.

Early on, our corner-back Sean Carey took out Olcan Laverty and was booked for it. I got in Sean's face and hit him a slap.

'Behave yourself,' I told him. 'You're no good to us on the bench!'

At least that's what Sean said I did. When he told me after the match, I couldn't remember doing it. I was obviously so nervous, but Sean told me it's the best thing I could have done, and he thanked me, because he was a bag of nerves too. To this day he tells me, 'You're the only boy who ever hit me and got away with it'.

We settled properly when Brendan Laverty scored our first goal, and we never looked back. Paddy Carey got another one just before half-time that put us six points up and, when 'Woody' scored another goal two minutes into the second-half, Ballycastle were *done*.

Everyone was hurling well, but Brendan Laverty was the man really running Ballycastle ragged. Every time we needed him that year, Brendan managed to come up trumps. He got our fifth goal straight after Seamus McNaughton got our fourth, and even though Ballycastle put a better look on the scoreboard late on, we knew from a fair way out that we were going to be Antrim champions.

Gilly McIlhatton was the hurling board chairman at that time, so it was him who handed me the cup. It was another proud moment, and the cue for some great celebrations. It was all back to The Pound, where we were running about and were probably getting big headed because everybody was patting us on the backs and telling us we were this and we were that… treating us like heroes.

But we enjoyed it. And you could see just how much it meant to Loughgiel people. One thing you can never doubt about Loughgiel people is their passion for hurling and their club – for good and bad. You could go out and win the championship and then lose the first league match the next year, and be called all the useless so-and-sos of the day.

That's the way it is with our supporters. They'll praise you to the heavens but won't be long telling you about it if things go wrong. It's good, because you don't rest on your laurels and it shows they care.

At some stage we were watching the video and Alec was commentating as a ball came down towards the side of my goals in the first-half. I ran over to it, stepped over it and let it go wide. On the video, Alec seemed incredibly impressed that I had the confidence to do something like that in the heat of the county final – step over a ball coming in and let it trickle wide.

The truth is I ran for the ball and missed it. It looked like I was selling a dummy a Brazilian footballer in that year's World Cup would have been proud of. No, I completely missed the thing.

THE ULSTER SEMI-FINAL against the Monaghan champions Clontibret was one to just tick off on our way to playing Ballygalget in the final. At least, that's what we thought.

We went down to Monaghan and were atrocious. We ended up winning easily but took most of the first-half to get to grips with the match and only pulled away after half-time. I managed to stand out on a day of things going badly. I was taking the penalties in training and would have knocked in 10 out of 10 every time, so Danny McMullan said, 'Right, any penalties, we'll bring Niall up to take them. PJ will go into goals, Paddy McIlhatton drops into full-back… and everyone moves back a spot to give him time to get back in goals.'

Danny obviously knew it was going to take me a while getting back.

So, we got a penalty against Clontibret but I missed the lift and had to set the ball down again with my hand. The referee missed it and the Clontibret boys were going mad. In hindsight, I'd rather the ref had spotted it.

They saved my penalty and put it out for a '65'. On the way back, I stopped and took the '65' and put it wide.

'That's you staying in goals!' said Danny.

Their captain gave 'Beaver' and Seamus McNaughton an awful tough time through the match, and afterwards he came in to our dressing room and let rip at us.

'ANTRIM CHAMPIONS?

'Yous are a disgrace. Coming down here and playing like that? We're a bunch of footballers… and that's the best yous could do?'

We didn't need to be told. If we played like that against Ballygalget in the Ulster final we wouldn't stand a chance. There was no way we were looking at All-Irelands or anything like it as we headed down to Ballygalget. We knew if we wanted an Ulster title, we'd have to earn it. That's the way it turned out and, for me, that was the toughest game we had all year.

'Beaver' got an early goal but then Ballygalget took over and we just couldn't get a foot-hold anywhere. It was hard and physical but there wasn't a dirty stroke and with Martin Bailie, Paddy Branniff and Seamus Fay – all class hurlers we knew well from the Antrim league – running things round the middle, we were lucky to go in a point ahead at half-time.

We just couldn't get by them.

Mick O'Connell was in the middle of the park and never hit a ball. Between them, the management made a switch and brought Mick in as a sweeper behind our half-back line, which I had never seen before. In those days it was one to 15… you kept your position and you hurled your man.

But it worked a treat. Mick turned everything in the second-half; we kept a two-man full-forward line and we won by goal.

« CHAPTER 5 »

BACK IN 1971, Loughgiel were the first-ever Ulster team to play in the All-Ireland club semi-final, in the first year of the competition. Munster champions Roscrea came up to Loughgiel and beat our great side, full of our greatest names. Now we were getting ready to host another Tipperary team for a place in the All-Ireland final.

After going up to Ballycastle to see great clubs like Blackrock and Ballyhale play in All-Ireland semi-finals, we got the chance to welcome Moycarkey-Borris to our home pitch. Even though we had home advantage, they were big favourites to beat us and were fancied to win the whole thing.

Their goalkeeper Tom Doran hadn't conceded a goal in the Munster Championship – him and their tough defence were the focus of all the write-ups before the match. They had beaten Patrickswell from Limerick in the Munster final, and were expected to come up and beat us without too much trouble.

The night before the match, I was playing over in the Lavey GAA social club in Derry. A fella there, James Convery, was up at every break slagging me, winding me up about the match.

'They're going to stuff yous tomorrow, Niall.'

'No, they won't. We're going to beat them, and not only that... they're not going to put one by me either.'

'All right, do you want a tenner on that?'

'Absolutely!'

The papers on the Monday said it had taken Moycarkey-Borris all of 15 seconds to earn James Convery his tenner.

The weather had been awful coming up to the match with the snow stopping just long enough to get the pitch cleared, but it was a still a horrible, wet, cold day for a match. And the pitch was like an ice-rink. Straight from the throw-in, the ball came up the middle of the field. Martin Carey came out for it but slipped and they got in for a goal.

A start like that, against the hot favourites, could have finished us. But the one thing that team didn't do all year was panic. Within five minutes we had wiped out their goal with points from 'Beaver', Aidan McNaughton and Brendan Laverty. After that, though, they got on top of us and we only managed one more point the rest of the half.

But we were still only a goal behind at half-time and we had hardly hurled at all. However, three points was a lot on a day and pitch like that. We kept things tight at the back but were finding it hard to make any headway up front.

They went four up, before Brendan Laverty got our first point of the second-half with just over 10 minutes left. Paddy Carey junior came on for Seamus McNaughton and he barely got his boots dirty before he scrambled in a goal that brought us level. Aidan McNaughton won the puckout and sent the ball back in towards their goal.

Doran could only block it out to 'Beaver' who smashed it into the net.

They were a beaten side, and they knew it. We'd gone from four points down to three points up in less than two minutes and there was no way we were going to lose it from there. In the end, we won by four after giving them that goal head-start. I'd lost my bet but I didn't care. Loughgiel were in the All-Ireland final.

Even though some of the Moycarkey-Borris fellas joked that when my dad and the selectors came to the hotel they were staying in before the match to welcome them to Antrim, they filled them with drink and that's why we won, they were great sportsmen and gracious in defeat.

Their selectors came into our dressing-room at the final and wished us all the best. And a few years later, when I was in Donegal for a golf trip, I had my guitar with me and played in one of the bars with a few of the others boys. A fella came up to me who I couldn't quite place.

'Niall?'

'Yes?'

'John McCormack… I was full-forward for Moycarkey-Borris and played against you in the semi-final in Loughgiel.'

One of the Stakelums who played for Tipperary was with him and every night until the end of the trip there were sing-songs together in the bar. One of the nights, I was chatting to John.

'You know, that was one dirty full-back you had,' he told me. 'He nearly put his stick up my backside.'

He obviously remembered PJ.

THE FINAL WAS meant to be two weeks later, but it would be two months before we got to play it, and even though the other semi-final was going on at the same time as ours, we wouldn't find out who our final opposition would be for another eight weeks.

The Offaly champions St Rynagh's had beaten Kiltormer from Galway in a match where four men were sent off. The problem was that after Declan Fogarty got his marching orders for St Rynagh's, he didn't march anywhere. He stayed on the pitch for another seven minutes before the referee realised he was still playing, and Kiltormer lodged an objection because St Rynagh's scored 1-2 while Fogarty was on when he shouldn't have been.

That was just the start of it.

Kiltormer were awarded the match but, straightaway, St Rynagh's appealed, saying Kiltormer had played an unregistered player. St Rynagh's won the appeal, but because both teams had seemingly broken the rules, did that mean they were both out and we were All-Ireland champions? To be honest we had no idea.

We kept training and trying to keep our focus, but it wasn't easy. We had gone from winning an All-Ireland semi-final, with a final to come a fortnight later, to not knowing when, where or even if the final would be played… with no idea who we'd play if it actually went ahead.

After St Rynagh's won their objection against Kiltormer they started another appeal – against the original decision to award the Galway side the match over Declan Fogarty staying on the pitch – to try to get back into the competition.

Central Council accepted St Rynagh's argument that Fogarty had only stayed on the pitch because he didn't realise he'd been sent off, and declared them the winners. There were rumblings that Kiltormer would take things further, maybe even to court, and by that stage we didn't know what to think.

Eventually, with less than a week's notice, it was official: We'd be playing St Rynagh's in the All-Ireland final.

The delay was difficult, but Danny McMullan was the perfect man to handle it. We had been training flat-out since Christmas, sometimes five nights a week and there was no way Danny was going to let all that work go to waste.

He brought in some different drills, just to lift us and keep it fresh when we could easily have lost interest because of what felt like the endless wait until the final.

After the semi-final more of the training was running, without realising we were running. In twos across the field, passing the ball... longer passes, shorter passes... until you were 10 yards from each other... drilling the ball, but on the move all the time.

It's standard stuff now, probably old hat even, but we had never done that before. Back then it was all slogs and sprints, before you moved on to your hurling training.

Danny kept plugging away at us, but within reason. He wasn't going to burn us out. There would be nights we'd do some drills and skills and be getting ready to start running and Danny would say. 'That's you boys... away yous go!' No hard running whatsoever.

I loved nights like that. He did that two or three times over the course of those two months. You had done a good hurling session and were ready to get into a real slog and... 'See you on Tuesday, boys!'

He knew when we needed that lift and that when we came back on Tuesday, he could put us through *anything*.

In the build-up to the semi-final, Danny had taken us to run up and down Corkey mountain above Loughgiel. You can imagine how much I loved that. It was a bad winter and a lot of the time you'd be tramping through snow, but those runs meant that by the time we had qualified for the final Danny could just keep us topped up, knowing the basic fitness was already there

Danny would have had us in groups of three up and down the field. I'd have one boy at my right side and another at my left side, and they'd have had a stick across my chest or my stomach and you'd start running a quarter-pace... and then

Danny would say, 'Right, pick it up to half pace!' And the sticks would be a wee bit tighter against you, and Danny would call for the pace to be upped again. And by the time you got into the other half, you were sprinting as they were holding you back with the stick.

You talk about putting strength into your legs! When it came to the last few minutes and you had to burst out of defence with the ball, you knew you had it in you.

I especially appreciated the fact he made sure I wasn't left behind in training. He wouldn't put me with someone like Mick O'Connell, who would leave me for dead. I was the sort of boy that if somebody ran away from me in training, that was it… I gave up. Danny put me in the position where I wouldn't give up and could get more out of myself. That kept us all going and kept us motivated.

When the snow was too deep on the mountain, Danny would have us on the pitch, sprinting from the pavilion to the end of the field. Between starting to train after Christmas and the All-Ireland final, I think we all took at least six seconds off our time to run from one end of the pitch to the other.

When you think of what can happen in the space of six seconds in a hurling match, that's a lot.

We took great pride in the fact that nobody was brought into the club from outside to train us or to coach us. We did it on our own. All the selectors were men from our club and we were blessed to have them.

It was a team effort and Danny, Dominic, Liam and my dad had great respect for each other and each other's opinions. Everybody had their say and their input. It's something that carried on through the years. The selectors always stood together on the line. Whenever things weren't going well, supporters used to complain that you'd see other teams with a selector up in the forward line and another down the other end or the far side of the field.

But our selectors were a team and made the big decisions collectively, so if a change needed to be made quickly, the men making the decision needed to be together.

Looking back, although the delay wasn't ideal, the uncertainty over who we were going to play probably helped us. During those two months we couldn't do anything but focus on ourselves. We couldn't get carried away worrying about the other team because we didn't know who the other team was! All we could do was get our own game right.

Part of that was challenge games we played against Glenariffe in the run-up to the semi-final and final. It wasn't just that they were the last team to beat us in a knockout match – in the previous year's Feis Cup – it was that my dad wanted any challenge match to let us work on our own game.

Glenariffe were a decent team that would let you play hurling, which meant you could try things out but still have it put it up to you. In my dad's mind, there was no point going down and playing Ballyhale Shamrocks or someone like that in a challenge game and maybe hitting a bad day and getting a whipping.

It just wouldn't do you any good and you'd be going into an All-Ireland semi-final with the confidence low from that beating you got down in Kilkenny or wherever.

His philosophy was to play a team you knew you could beat, and have the freedom to try different tactics against them but still be aware that, on a bad day, or if you took it too easy, they could turn you over.

People in Loughgiel should be grateful to Glenariffe. They always made themselves available and we must have played them three or four times in challenge games. Between the Feis Cup and those matches, Glenariffe had a big bearing on us winning the All-Ireland.

THE FINAL WAS set for Croke Park.

The night before, we stayed in The Clarence Hotel by the Liffey. I was used to going down to Dublin for matches with the county but it was different with the club. I'd been away plenty of times with the Antrim minors and the seniors, but this was my first time away with the boys I grew up with.

We went for a walk up O'Connell Street and then into a big snooker hall across the river from the hotel, where we played and sat and chatted. We had never done anything like that before. I remember just sitting back and looking around at the boys… and taking it all in. I never said anything but just thought… *God, this is great.*

I felt so proud to be down there with my club.

I was 20, we were a young team and I thought that this would be the way of things to come… but it didn't happen. You thought you were going to be down there every year, but that was the only one.

I'm glad I appreciated it when I did.

EVERYTHING SEEMED TO go wrong for us until the very end of the final. Aidan McNaughton missed frees he'd normally knock over in his sleep, then Mick O'Connell moved onto them and hit them wide as well.

In the second-half Mick had a penalty saved too.

I was blocked down twice as I was trying to clear the ball out on the end-line and, both times, the umpire gave a '65' that Padraig Horan scored.

Martin Coyle had scored a great point to get us up and running, but I think we were too nervous, especially in the first-half. Brendan Laverty did score a goal after five minutes but we should have been far further ahead when, just before half-time, I made a save but the ball bounced out off the post… straight to their corner-forward, who buried it.

That meant they were just two down at half-time and, within a minute of the second-half, they were ahead thanks to a carbon copy goal. Another save… another ball off the post… another grateful St Rynagh's man on the edge of the square.

Those two goals were their first scores from play and, all of a sudden, we were chasing the game. But the frees still wouldn't go over and when Mick missed his penalty, it just didn't look like it was going to be our day.

Paddy Carey junior had come on as a sub and was our third free-taker of the day. Thankfully, he was able to put over our equaliser with three minutes left. But there was time for one more free, and for our luck to change.

With time virtually up, Horan stood over the ball about 50 yards out from my goal. It never occurred to me that he would miss.

I asked the umpire how long was left and he told me there was less than a minute. I asked him for a ball and I had it in my hand as Padraig bent to lift his ball out the field. We were about to be a point down, so I'd needed to get the ball as far down the field as I could… as quickly as I could.

But I never got the chance. As soon as the ball passed the posts the whistle went for full-time and, thank God, Padraig had hit it wide.

Even though we had been let off the hook, I sat in the Croke Park changing room gutted that we hadn't won the final. We had dominated so much of the match, especially in the first-half, that it felt we had missed the boat and we'd never get a better chance. I'm sure I wasn't the only one who thought that.

But, the next day, it was a different story. My head was up again, we were back training at the pitch and no one was thinking about what might have been. I was buzzing – and convinced we were going to win it.

The replay was a week later at Casement. The county board had made the case that because the first match was played in Leinster – at Croke Park – then the replay should come to Ulster.

It honestly wouldn't have bothered us if we had to go back to Croke Park. I loved it – it was my favourite ground from the first day I was in it as an under-16 – and I didn't think it was any advantage for St Rynagh's to be playing there.

But I didn't realise at that stage just how special the following Sunday at Casement would be. I couldn't believe it when we got to the ground and there were 10,000 people in there. As well as our own supporters, the place was packed with gaels from all over Antrim – but especially Belfast.

When it came to Dunloy or Ballycastle the rivalry was so fierce you could hardly guarantee they would want us to win – and vice versa. If wasn't really like that with the Belfast clubs. Belfast people would come out and support any team representing Antrim.

Paddy McIhatton was one of the veterans on the team. He had played on the great team of the late-60s and early-70s and was still one of our most important players at centre-back. While we took a break from training for a couple of months after we won the Ulster title, Paddy trained away on his own, doing 20 laps of the field two or three nights a week because he knew at his age that he wouldn't be able to keep up with the younger boys.

It's one thing to keep running when you've a man beside you or one in front of you, but to do that on his own in the depths of winter shows how much he was prepared to give to that team.

Seconds into the replay, he had already given a fair amount of skin to the Loughgiel cause. Virtually straight from the throw-in he cleared a ball away just before Padraig Horan got his pull in and clattered Paddy on the leg, skinning him from his ankle to his knee. His shin was raw and I immediately thought… *We're in serious bother here, this man's not going to be fit to play an hour like that.* But, of course, he did, and he gave Horan, Offaly's great All-Ireland winning captain, his fill of it.

Any time I'd be talking to Padraig, he'd always ask me, 'How's the wee man with the band?'… because Paddy had long hair and he wore a white headband. Padraig never forgot coming up against him.

We controlled the match from start to finish. Whereas almost everything had gone wrong for us in the drawn game, almost everything went right in the replay. That wasn't quite showing up on the scoreboard, however, and we were a point behind after about 20 minutes. But we had been hurling well and it looked to us that they didn't really have much more to show us.

When Brendan Laverty got a ball and went past three defenders before thumping it past Damien Martin, we knew we were on our way. That gave us a three-point lead at half-time, and with the way our defence was playing, it already looked like being enough.

They had a fella, Dermot Devery, a young lad with long hair who was a real runner and dangerman. Eamonn Connolly was on him and just ran and ran and never gave him a minute's peace. He just chased and *chased*. At one stage Devery simply ran the ball out over the end-line... Eamonn had chased him from the pitch.

At midfield, Mick O'Connell and Gerard McKinley moved every ball on the ground, constantly keeping the St Rynagh's defence under pressure. They had to deal with ball after ball, and they just couldn't settle.

I WAS DOWN at the Railway Cup with Ulster before the first match and got chatting to Noel Skehan. I was talking to him about us being in the All-Ireland final and I was asking him for advice.

He said Leinster teams like to get the ball and run at you, and the best way to beat a team from Leinster is to play first-time hurling... keep the ball moving.

That was our style anyway – and had been Loughgiel's traditional style of play. Ground hurling, fast moving... get it up the pitch as quickly as possible and trust your forwards to do the damage.

AND OUR FORWARDS were on song that afternoon.

Brendan Laverty was giving Aidan Fogarty problems, and his goal was just the latest big moment he gave us that season.

'Woody' was causing havoc at left half-forward with his runs in from the wing and from one of those the ball broke across to 'Beaver' who buried it to the net. We were five points up with 10 minutes left, and we knew we were going to be All-Ireland champions. They scored a goal from a penalty with virtually the last puck of the game, but it didn't matter.

All of a sudden, the pitch was a sea of red and white. You could barely move for people. It was only when I watched a video of the match later that I saw my dad running onto the pitch in his suit – a happy, *happy* man.

It was just mayhem. I can't remember what I said after I lifted the cup, but I know I was so overcome I forgot to the ask for the traditional 'Three Cheers' for St Rynagh's. I couldn't hang around because I was told I had to get home to do a live interview with Mick Dunne for RTE radio later that night.

Someone drove me home and, after the interview, I waited down at Hughie's Corner for the bus and the cup to head into Loughgiel.

If the celebrations in The Pound were big after the county final, you could multiply them by whatever you want for the All-Ireland. It didn't close its doors for a week… day or night.

I've never taken a drink, but I had always said that if we won the All-Ireland, I would get full that night in The Pound. But when it came to it, I didn't need a drink.

That feeling was enough. I just stood in The Pound and soaked it all in. I wanted to remember that feeling forever.

A FEW MONTHS later, Rasharkin officially opened their new pitch. Dunloy played Kilrea in a football match, but the main attraction was Rasharkin bringing Kiltormer up to play us. Unofficially, our All-Ireland title was on the line.

I'm sure they were up for a good weekend, but it was obvious they had come up with something to prove too. They thought it should have been them in the All-Ireland final against us, and now they had their chance to show what they would have done if they had got the chance.

Instead, we went out and completed the clean-sweep of provincial champions. We'd beaten Munster and Leinster, and now we'd beaten Connacht too.

My first hurling memory was in Rasharkin, and now I was standing in Rasharkin as the captain of Loughgiel Shamrocks… the undisputed All-Ireland champions.

PART **THREE**

'This is what puts a roof over your head!'

I've come a long way on my musical journey through life and have met so many fantastic people along the way.

Music and hurling have been my life, and have made me the man I am today. I've been lucky to work with so many talented musicians. Here we are as Irish Gold... Bill Cushley, myself, Pandy Walshe and Mickey Kerr. And as The Hatfield and McCoys (from left) Brendan McGarritty, Pandy Walshe, Tracey McAuley, myself, Eamonn Loughran and Rod McAuley. Brendan McGarritty sadly passed in early 2022.

Recording Jim Nelson's Men with Francis Lochlin, Norman McGreer and Brian Boyle. Brian and Francis were in The Kathy Kane Band with me, and the four of us played together in The Leanne Rivera Band.

« CHAPTER 6 »

MY FIRST GUITAR wasn't really my own. It belonged to Fr Hugh Mullan, our parish priest, who used to come into the primary school and sing to us – his big number was… *There Was An Old Woman Who Swallowed A Fly*.

I ended up with his acoustic guitar, but only after it belonged to my brother Anthony first. My dad bought it for him, but he stopped playing and I picked it up. I haven't put down a guitar since. Straightaway, I knew I loved it. I went to six guitar lessons, learned the chords, and then just picked up the rest myself by ear.

Even before I picked up an instrument, I'd loved music. There was a television programme on in the late-60s called *Tommy's Toy Shop*, hosted by Tommy James. He would sit and play the piano while children would come on and sing a song. The teachers sent me up to the studio in Belfast to sing, and I sang… *The Black Velvet Band*. Then you went to a window in the toy shop and you picked out a toy that went to a child who was sick in hospital.

Any money I got would be spent on records and, once I got my guitar, I'd sit watching *Top of the Pops* and try to play along. It was the early-70s and I loved the glam rock stuff – The Sweet, Slade and T Rex. I couldn't tell you how many hours I spent trying to learn *Mouldy Old Dough* by Lieutenant Pigeon.

My dad bought me my next guitar – a Shaftesbury copy of a Fender telecaster. It cost £18 and that was the guitar I played at my first-ever gig, in The Cabin bar in Ballymena when I was 14. My first wage was £4 and I knew exactly what I was going to do with it.

I saved every penny I got until, when I was 17, I bought myself a Fender Stratocaster that cost £402. And it was the full £402... there was no £2 off it.

I still have it to this day and it still sounds great.

I was happy to spend £402 on a guitar when I was 17 in 1979 because I already knew that music was what I wanted to do.

DURING THE SUMMER holidays, when I was 14, I went to do roadie for Leo McCafferty and The Glensmen, who were a big showband at the time. Seamus Richmond was the band leader and fiddle player, and my dad knew Seamus would look after me out on the road. And he did – he took me under his wing as we travelled all over the country – and England and Scotland too – maybe five, six nights a week during the holidays.

That was the start of nearly 10 good years playing with Seamus in the music scene, as well as the last years of his career on the hurling pitch. When Seamus was playing, I would have gone to the match with him... then drove with him to a gig. I remember going down to Gortin Glen in Tyrone one night, after Loughgiel had played Glenariffe in the Feis Cup.

Seamus had got a bat on the hand and by the time we got down there his hand was the size of a balloon. Seamus was the fiddle player in the band and never missed a note even though his hand was twice the size it should have been.

I'd just be there to set up the gear and then, when the band was playing, I'd be down on the floor listening to them. Seeing them up on stage and the reaction they were getting from the crowd made up my mind... *This is what I want to do.*

If I was starry-eyed when I joined the county hurling panel, I was the same when I went out on the road with the band. I played my guitar and was happy enough to try to get better at that, but these boys were all swapping instruments and playing just as well on each one of them. I was so impressed.

The piano player would go onto bass, the bass player would swap with him... Seamus would play fiddle... then go over and play guitar. It's probably why I tried to learn different instruments as I was growing up – I was just amazed at the musicians being able to do that.

One night, the band was playing in the Lilac Ballroom in Carndonagh in

Donegal. The boys were all down at the hotel, having a drink before the show. The gear was all set up, the hall was packed and the people from the ballroom came up to the hotel.

'Leo, we're looking for you to get started here… the hall's full.'

Leo was having a good time, signing autographs, and just talking to boys in the bar. So, he said, 'Sure, yous take Niall with you… go up and do an hour before we go on'.

So, I went up and played acoustic guitar and sang a few songs. That was my first time playing to a packed hall like that. I'd been on a stage with concerts at school and wee bars but this was a real buzz.

TRAVELLING WITH LEO and the band had other perks too. We were over in Manchester for some concerts round St Patrick's Day and, on the morning, Seamus shook me out of bed.

'Right, up for Mass!'

It was early and I was in no form to be going to Mass that morning.

'Get up. It's a Holy Day of Obligation!'

'Maybe it is in Ireland… but not over here.'

'It's a Holy Day… everywhere. GET UP!'

So, I got up and we headed to Mass. On the way back we went past Old Trafford.

'Stop the van!'

I was going to make a pilgrimage of my own. We went into the shop and I bought a couple of wee things and we had a look around outside to see if we could get into the stadium. Then a big man, he must have been 6'8", wearing a suit came over to us. He had heard us talking.

'Ah lads, yous are over from Ireland?'

'Aye, we're over playing with The Leo McCaffrey Band.'

'Leo? I know Leo, come in with me!'

It turned out he was one of the Manchester United directors. He took us up to the canteen and there was Dave Sexton, the manager, and some of the players sitting having breakfast. We got our breakfast too – at the other side of the room – and were taken on a tour of Old Trafford.

We got down to the pitch and I said, 'I'd love to take a bit home'.

'Good luck!' said our new director friend. 'But if any of those boys catch you,' he added, pointing to the groundsmen, 'You better be ready to run!'

I took my chance and dug out a wee bit of the pitch. Sure enough, we had to run for our lives out of Old Trafford.

THE McGURKS, WHO took fun-fairs and amusements all over Ireland, used to keep their rides and equipment up near our house in Cloughmills over the winter, where they'd set up their stuff, and clean and paint and test it, to get it ready for going back on the road during the summer.

One of the family, Colly McGurk, had been a singer in The Fairways Showband, a big pop band at the time. She actually gave me my first guitar lessons and she had the idea to set up a band to play around the local pubs. My cousin Aloysious was a drummer – he ended up playing with Susan McCann – and he came in along with one of my good friends, Donal Carey, whose father had played on that old Cloughmills hurling team with my dad.

That was my first band. Just a wee group of youngsters playing music.

Later on, Barry Mulholland, God rest him, approached me saying he wanted to put together a bigger band and do everything properly. He'd buy us suits so we'd look the part and things would be done professionally.

The Glensmen had just finished, so Seamus Richmond came on board along with Frankie McBride and Ciaran McHugh. When Barry had to give up the band because of work commitments, Manus Marron came in to drum with us. He'd been playing with Gloria, who had a massive hit with *One Day at a Time* and I learned a hell of lot from Manus.

Back then, when I played lead guitar, I just played lead guitar over *everything*, but Manus told me, 'No, just play it straight. Do your solos, do your intros but get in, get out… do your part, let everyone else do theirs!'

Manus had played in the bigger showbands and was a real pro. At that stage, I was working full-time in the shop and trying to play when I could with the band. Getting to learn from people like Manus, who ran the band as well, was brilliant.

The band was called Country Cream, before we brought in Kathy Kane to sing and became the Kathy Kane Band. That was my band for seven or eight years, and when Manus retired, I took over the running of it.

Towards the end, Kathy was about to get married and we didn't know if she'd be staying with the band on not, and some things were getting to me about the band as well.

A friend of mine from school, his sister was getting married and we were playing the wedding. The reception was running way behind time and the fella who was the drummer at the time said, 'I've got to go, I've a party to go to in Ballycastle!'

'We can't go until this is over.'

So, he drummed away for another 10 minutes and then got up… 'I'm going!'

'You can't go in the middle of someone's wedding… if you're going, then don't be coming back!'

That helped make up my mind that I was done with it. I thought, *Right, Kathy's getting married and this will come to an end.*

We were supposed to play at the wedding of Eamonn O'Hara, who was a sports reporter for *The Irish News*. Antrim were playing in a league match down in Offaly and Eamonn was covering it and I had to tell him, 'Sorry, Eamonn but the band's split up and we can't do your wedding'.

Eamonn worked alongside Tony McGee in the paper's sports department and Tony also wrote a country music column. The next week it was in the paper that the Kathy Kane Band had split up. The problem was that Kathy didn't know about it. I don't know what happened, whether it was crossed wires or something else.

When I got back from the Offaly match, I got a call from the piano player and the bass player to say we've got another girl to front the band, if you and the drummer can sort out your differences. I said it was fine, but somebody else would have to take on running the band. I was busy in the shop, and running the band as well as playing was too much.

I said, 'I'll keep playing, but that's it!'

So, we started again as Leanne and the Riviera Band.

We had been playing for about three weeks and Kathy, who had come home from her honeymoon, landed at McGinn's in Ballintoy where we did a lot of work. The atmosphere was serious and I got the blame for it.

'I left the band, then these boys phoned me… and said they had no singer, so I came back,' I explained.

'It was in the paper… this is your fault!' Kathy replied.

'I didn't even know that was in the paper,' I said. She wasn't having any of it.

I met Kathy in the Manor Hotel in Ballymoney about a year later. We passed outside the toilets and she hit me with her shoulder as she went by. Things were that bad.

We were really close and that hurt me but, thankfully, it got cleared up and the most important thing is that we're still good friends.

IN THE SAME way I could learn different things from watching and being around great hurlers through my career, I was lucky to have the same experience in music. I could also really enjoy myself. I played with Peter O'Hara, who had left The Indians, and we were on the road together for some great times.

He was unreal, a great showman. He was full of devilment and always had a big smile on him.

When I started with Peter, I remember saying that we had to get changed into our suits. But there were no suits!

'That's the only suit you need!' he said, as he flashed a big smile.

When we played The Pound in Loughgiel the place was packed every Saturday night and it wasn't because of me. Peter was just fabulous. I was playing piano and guitar at that time, and Peter was doing the same.

Whenever Peter was in The Indians, *Apache*, the Shadows hit, was their big show-stopper. One night in The Pound, Peter had the idea to get Brendan McGarry – 'Chopper', a great hurler, who would play for Loughgiel – up to play. He was only a youngster at the time and when he came up, I handed him my guitar.

Peter was hidden out of sight and started playing *Apache* while young 'Chopper' was playing along... pretending it was him. Everybody was stunned and when the song finished, they crowded round 'Chopper'.

'God, I didn't know you played guitar.'

Another night we were supposed to be starting at nine o'clock and by half nine there was still no sign of Peter – and he needed to be there to get the gear out. So, I started ringing round the bars in Ballymena to ask if anyone had seen him.

'Aye, he was here a while ago, but I've no idea where he is now.'

I was starting to panic because the place was packed. Then I heard a big commotion out the back... and there was Peter. I got him into the place and started pouring coffee into him. By this stage it was ten o'clock and everybody was getting impatient.

'Come on, Peter... we have to get out here!'

'Hang on, I've to go for a run first.'

So, he disappeared out the back door and I heard this clattering. I went out to see what was going on and there were mops and buckets lying everywhere, but no sign of Peter. Out of nowhere, he appeared.

'Right, let's go!'

The hands were completely skinned off him.

'Did you fall, Peter?'

'Not at all.'

I've never seen a performance like the one he gave that night. He had them dancing on top of the tables from start to finish.

You could never be sure what way Peter was going to go with music. If he came in one day and said, 'Right, that's me finished,' it wouldn't have surprised you. The same as if he'd come in and said, 'Right, I've found us a singer'.

That's what happened when he found a girl from Belfast who had moved to Ballymena and, all of a sudden, we were a pop band called Heatwave, doing chart stuff.

That lasted about a year before Peter did say, 'Right, that's me finished!'

I ALWAYS WONDERED what I would do when I stopped playing hurling.

It was such a big part of my life, the *biggest* part of my life at that time. As far as possible, work had to fit around it, whether it was in the factory or later in the shop. And my other 'work' – though I never saw it as that – music also had to take a back seat.

Sometimes, there was a conflict. I missed the 1986 championship because I was so busy with the music that I just couldn't give the commitment to train every night with the county.

But almost every time there was a decision to be made, hurling was given the priority. There were times down through the years when I was offered the chance to join bigger bands and devote more time to music, but as long I was hurling that wasn't really an option.

Whenever I was starting to hurl for the senior county team and I'd have been playing on a Saturday night, Fergus McNaughton and his wife Maureen would have been sitting outside the gig, waiting for me to finish. I'd get into the car, maybe talk for a while... then sleep as we drove to Cork or Waterford or places like that.

That's how I started off my county career, but if there was a really big conflict, hurling got the nod.

When I did finally hang up my boots, I was lucky that I had already found myself in probably the best musical place I had ever been.

I was playing with Walter Lewis, who used to have his own big showband, and a singer Shirley Kyle, and was really enjoying it. Then Andy 'Pandy' Walshe approached me to join forces with him, as the fella he was playing with was leaving at the end of the year.

Whenever I was playing in the Kathy Kane Band, I used to go over to Maghera on a Sunday night when 'Pandy' was playing with Philomena Quinn. I always loved his singing. It turns out that whenever we were playing, he used to come in and hear me. Though we didn't know that about one another when we started together.

About a year in we sort of admitted that we'd always been mutual fans. So, whenever he asked me if I'd be interested in playing with him, I took the hand off him. I told Walter I'd stay with him until the end of the year and Walter, like the gentleman he was, was happy with that.

We played our first gig on New Year's Night in 1993 as a two-piece, Road Crew, and that became the next 15 years of my life. I'd been playing music for nearly 20 years already but I learned so much from my time with Road Crew. That was because of the level of musicians we were playing with, but also because, after stopping hurling later that year, I had so much more time to devote to it.

About six weeks after we started playing, daddy died. I had already retired from the county and finished up that season with Loughgiel before stopping altogether.

When we started, 'Pandy' told me if he got a year out of me, he would be happy. I had been doing maybe two nights a week and weekends, but when he landed, he had a diary for the year sitting full, a minimum of five days a week. Once we got started and got established it was regularly a seven nights a week thing.

There was one period of six months when we had two nights off. We had five nights a week in bars and concerts, and then weddings on Friday and Saturday. There were plenty of times that we did more than one gig a day... and we were playing all over the north.

Playing with 'Pandy' in Road Crew was like a musical education.

This was when, in my mind, I really learned how to play music properly. It was like hurling. You won't get any better if you just train maybe once a week or only play a match at the weekend. You have to be doing it *all* the time. That's how you hone your skills, how your playing gets tighter, and how you learn to play with other people in a team.

And when you're playing with people of a higher standard, you learn from them, too, and you improve yourself.

In my 15 years in Road Crew I got to play with some great people from different bands, and was doing it around places like Tyrone that are full of a lot of great musicians. It took me to a new level. The great bonus – maybe the *most* important thing – is that I got to meet some lovely, *lovely* people through the music scene. Even though they were in a different league to me, they were nice, generous and welcoming. I had a great time playing with the likes of Dan O'Hara, God rest him, backing Philomena Begley.

Willie Loughrey, who performed as Rock Stewart, would come out and see us with his wife Catherine; he's a lovely man to be around. He could keep up the show off stage as well. One night, we had played in Omagh and were driving back when we saw what looked like a red light flashing. We thought we were being pulled over by the police, but it was Willie, standing at the side of a road waiting for us to come along so he could give us a scare.

IT WASN'T JUST the musicians.

You got to know bar and hotel owners who went above and beyond to treat us well. Henry Downey, who was the Derry captain when they won the All-Ireland title in 1993, approached us to play in his bar in Magherafelt. The bar was doing nothing on a Sunday night with maybe half a dozen people in it, very quiet.

He asked us to come into the bar and do a residency. Straightaway, I said, 'No'. I wasn't interested. We tried that sort of thing before and it didn't work. It was too restrictive, as it ruled out other Sunday night gigs.

'Pandy' went back to Henry and told him I wasn't interested. Henry came back. 'I'll give you six months' money up front and if it doesn't work… just walk away, no hard feelings.'

So, we decided to give it a go.

At the start, there were the same half-dozen people in the bar as always. We started and then that became a dozen, and got up to around 20 and Henry was already happy.

Sometimes, a couple of people in the bar would come up and do a song and 'Pandy', who was a great man for organising things, had the idea of starting a competition. At that time, *I'm A Celebrity, Get Me Out of Here* was the big programme on a Sunday night so we started a singing competition… *I'm a Slabber-ity, What Am I Doing Here?* It caught on and the bar started to fill up and, next thing, there were 50 people in just to see what this thing was about. To give it a push, Henry talked to his suppliers and came up with a £1,000 holiday as a prize.

After that, it took off. There were heats over the course of a few weeks and, by the time it got to the semi-final, there was maybe 400 people at it. When the final came around you couldn't move in the place. The finalists got a limousine ride to a meal, there was a champagne reception… Rock Stewart was a guest judge for the final. We had about six years of that when Sunday nights were booming in Downey's bar in Magherafelt. Henry was more than good to us and gave us plenty of work in his place in Derry too.

We did a lot of work with Mickey McIlhatton and the Greenvale Hotel in Cookstown. We seemed to be playing weddings there every weekend and every Christmas there was party after party. We brought out an album in 1993 and Mickey gave us the money the make the CD. We had a big night in his hotel to launch it and you had Brendan Quinn, Rock Stewart, Philomena Begley… all the top acts came and did a bit for us free of charge.

We cleared three and a half thousand pounds and gave the money to Mickey, to pay him back for bank-rolling the album. He was counting through the money and we thought he was checking it to make sure it was all there, but he handed us back two thousand pounds.

'Here! I had a good night and yous earned this!'

They were the sort of boys… great men, who helped my musical career.

WE WERE FRIENDLY with another band called Goldseal, with Mickey Kerr, Sean Hutchinson and Billy Cushley – and we would occasionally get together to do some joint sessions. In 1996, we all got the chance to go out to Chicago for three weeks of gigs.

About two weeks before we left, I was named as the goalkeeper on a team picked to celebrate the 25th anniversary of the All-Ireland Club Championships. Unfortunately, the presentation ceremony was scheduled for when I was due to be out in Chicago, as we would be out there for St Patrick's Day. I sent word down to Dublin to say I was sorry, but I couldn't make the presentation as I was in America.

We headed out and were staying in the house of the fella who owned the bar where we were playing every night. At eleven o'clock in the morning we headed to the bar, which was already busy. Unsurprisingly, a couple of the boys started on the drink, but that wasn't on the table for me… so I just played pool and darts all day, killing time before we went on that night.

The next day, we were up and headed down to the bar again at eleven o'clock and it was obvious that this was going to be what it was like for the three weeks.

I'm not doing this every day, I thought to myself. *I'm going home!*

There's only so much pool and darts you can play. So, I phoned Naomi, my girlfriend at the time, now my wife, to see if she could get down to Shannon to lift me from the airport if I came home early. The problem was, I had to get on a phone in the house of the fella who was paying me to stay out there, without him knowing what I was planning.

As I was talking to Naomi, she asked, 'How do I get to Shannon?'

But she never got to finish the question before I had to put down the phone in case your man heard me.

Flights to Ireland were rammed, with it being around St Patrick's Day, and the only one I could get on was with Aeroflot, the Russian airline that had a flight that stopped at Shannon to refuel.

There was hardly anyone on it and not a word of English anywhere. It was as rough a flight as I ever had in my life. I was counting the minutes until we touched down in Shannon, and was never as glad to be back home.

The following week, there was a thing on the TV about Aeroflot and its planes. It told stories of captains letting their sons come up and fly the plane, of pilots being drunk from before take-off to well after landing. There was a woman on who said she sat down with her husband only to find that she didn't have a seatbelt. So, he swapped seats with the wife so she would have a seatbelt, but when the plane took off they found out it wouldn't have made much difference as the seats weren't bolted to the floor.

If I'd known that, I would have stayed in America.

I managed to get home in time for the ceremony and was able to pick up my award. Then I got a phone call from 'Pandy'.

'You'll never guess who was here looking for you?'

'Who?'

'Marty Morrissey!'

Marty Morrissey was over in Chicago doing something else with RTE and because they thought I was there and couldn't make it back to Ireland to get my award, he had shown up at the bar to do a story with me.

Little did he know that at that same time I was probably halfway across the Atlantic, saying a wee prayer I'd make it back to Ireland.

AFTER I FINISHED with Road Crew I really didn't fancy going out on my own. I liked to be in the background and 'Pandy' was the perfect man to have out in front. I didn't mind singing but he had the gift of the gab and could do everything you needed to do as a front man, which suited me.

It just never occurred to me to either front a band or be up on stage on my own. My mum's cousin Robert Darragh had left the band he was in, so I went along with him for a couple of years but it wasn't paying because it was only really one night at week.

Eventually, I started going out on my own because I had no choice. I started with one night a week, then two, and my confidence built up to the point where I thought I could maybe do this by myself. I got to the point where I was out five nights a week and more.

All this time, I was still working in the shop. I never saw music as a job because I enjoyed it so much, but I was basically working two full-time jobs.

My brother Anthony died of cancer in 2014. Around the same time, my brother Jarlath and sister Maggie were going through health issues too, and when Anthony came and told me he had only a few weeks left it was a real wake-up call. I was in the shop from half-five, six in the morning, getting the papers in, writing out the orders… and then doing hot food for the fellas in vans who would come in in the mornings.

My sister Maggie would come in at eight o'clock and I'd go to bed from maybe nine to eleven, and then be back in the shop until six o'clock. Then at seven, I was away playing music. I told Naomi I was done. Everything was work, *work… work* and I felt like we'd done nothing as a family. I wasn't going to let that go on any longer. That's when I knew I'd have to close the shop and just have one job, and get back quality time to spend with my family.

I went full-time with the music and I've been playing ever since.

IN FEBRUARY 2020 I was having some trouble with my throat and went to the doctor, and they discovered some nodules. I had done something like 60 gigs in December and January, and I was told that I'd have to stop singing until they were sorted out. I said that wasn't an option because singing was my living.

Then Covid came along, and I had no choice.

Like so much else in the world, music stopped. Pubs closed, weddings were cancelled and live music was banned. It turned out to be a good thing for my throat – when I went back for a check-up about nine months later, they found that one side had completely cleared up.

There was still a nodule and swelling on the other side, and because my voice is my livelihood, I was booked in for an operation to get it sorted.

I doubt there'll be such a simple fix for the music industry. I definitely can't see me playing 60 gigs in the space of two months again. The pandemic has changed things so much. Every bar owner has had to look at how much it's worth to have someone in playing live music. Even when restrictions were lifted, a lot of places didn't reopen, or didn't renew their entertainment licence.

The amount of work that existed before just won't be there again.

At the start of October 2021, I filled in my diary for gigs for 2022… and there weren't 40. The last October before Covid my diary would have had 150 gigs in it for the following year, and that number only grew and grew. It's the same for everyone in the business.

I didn't put the instruments away entirely during the pandemic. I've known James McGarrity for a long time. His father Brendan was a drummer who played in a lot of bands I crossed paths with down the years, and James has his own band Keltic Storm, as well as being a massive promoter of shows and concerts. President Michael D Higgins praised James for the work he did during the pandemic keeping Irish country music going and helping musicians financially – and it was well deserved.

He put on concerts that were broadcast over the internet with a big name headlining and then a few others at my level playing and it was a huge help – not just financially but for keeping artists' names out there. I also found it kept my head right. Being told, all of sudden, that you can't do something you've done all your life hit me for six… never mind the fact it's what pays the bills.

James, who also helped me get an Arts Council grant which I didn't think I was entitled to, softened the blow for me and a huge number of musicians.

I'VE GOT MUSIC to thank for giving me the best thing in my life – my family. I was playing piano with 'Pandy' in the front bar of Clubland in Cookstown in 1994 when I met Naomi.

Five years later, we got married in St Lucia in the Caribbean. The 11th of November… 11-11. Thankfully, easy to remember. We were supposed to be married at eleven o'clock down on the beach at the place we were staying, but just before it was time to head down the heavens opened and we had to wait until three o'clock to finally tie the knot.

Poor Naomi was up in the room from eleven in her wedding dress. I was down playing pool.

'How's Niall?' she asked.

'He's grand – he's down there with the lads playing pool.'

She wasn't impressed.

We had gone away to get married because Naomi's mum had died a couple of years before and with daddy gone as well, we decided we didn't want a wedding at home – that it would be best to head off somewhere.

The reception was planned for the Greenvale Hotel in Cookstown a couple of days after the wedding. But the rain that had postponed the wedding had been coming ahead of a hurricane, and we couldn't fly home on time.

First, we flew to Barbados and stayed there for one night, but we were still scheduled to get back in time for the reception. But the hurricane was still blowing and I had to ring Mickey McIlhatton and tell him we weren't going to be back.

'Grand!' said Mickey. 'I'll ring you back.'

Between Mickey and my wife's sister, we managed to get the word out to everyone that the reception was being moved to the Monday night. Some people had to go home to England and six people from Cookstown turned up on

Saturday night anyway because they thought it was a joke, but on the Monday evening we had about 260 guests with us for our wedding reception.

I didn't want it to just be a band up playing and trying to get everyone up on the dance-floor – the usual sort of thing – so I had the comedian Gene Fitzpatrick on first.

Gene went on and did an hour. Very clean, very funny, something everyone could enjoy. Back then Gene was doing weddings for £700 and when I asked him if he could do ours, he said, 'Give me £200 Niall… just don't tell anybody'. I thought that was so good of him.

And then, when I went out to pay him after the show, he wouldn't take a penny off me. You meet really good guys through the business.

Maurice Crum played a bit with his band, and 'Pandy' and I did an hour ourselves, and then we had a disco at the end of the night. I'd have preferred it if we hadn't played but Naomi wanted her family to see what I did. A lot of her family knew I played music but they hadn't heard me.

So, I was just told I was doing it and I did it. Start as you mean to go on…

It was a great night, and I look back at the video sometimes and it brings back nothing but good memories. Mum enjoyed it too, but I know she was worried when the wedding was coming up because it meant I'd be moving out of the house. Even though we were moving into a house not 50 yards away, just behind the home place, it was a big change for her to take, especially with daddy being gone.

We had missed the reception on the Saturday, and I said to Naomi I would stay with mum on the Sunday night. I think that *settled* mum. I came in and it was a relief to her, it showed that I would never be far away. The following night at the wedding she was in bits, crying, but they were tears of joy. She loved it, and Naomi's dad was the same.

Before we were going to get the plane to go to St Lucia, I was waiting for Naomi and had to go in and see where she was? I found her out the back, hugging her dad. The pair of them were in tears. Those are the things that are really important.

WE WANTED TO start a family as soon as we could, and Rhiannon was born in August 2000. Naomi didn't want Rhiannon to be an only child – she thought she'd be spoiled – and Sharelle was born a year and a day after her sister. Three years later, Ashdyn came along. Three girls in the house, all of them spoiled rotten. I always said I'd never spoil my children but when they came along, I couldn't help it.

None of the girls are interested in sport. They take that from their mum. She can't understand the appeal and I try to explain, it but she's not convinced.

Ashdyn did briefly play camogie for the primary school and they got into an Ulster final. We went over to watch them and I got the shock of my life. I nearly had to put Naomi into the car. She's so mild-mannered but that day when she saw her daughter getting bumped around and the sticks flying around her, she was ready to hop the wire.

She couldn't have anybody hitting her daughter. At half-time she went up to Ashdyn and told her, 'You start swinging that thing round you!'

'Don't be saying that,' I said.

'No, you look after yourself.'

And that was that!

Of the three, Ashdyn would probably be the most into playing music. She listens to everything too. She might come in singing something from the 60s or 70s and it would surprise me that she's into that sort of thing.

I tried to teach her guitar when she was younger and she didn't want to know. Now she sits and plays guitar and piano in her bedroom. She's completely self-taught and she puts me to shame. I'll hear her play a chord and stop. *I couldn't play that,* I'd think.

She started to listen to a bit of country but would laugh at me for playing it. I'd be singing country songs and she'd say, 'Dad, don't be singing that!'

But I have to tell her… 'This is what puts a roof over your head, pet!'

« CHAPTER 7 »

THE VERY FIRST thing it says in the GAA Official Guide – after telling you what the association's name is – is that it's a… 'National Organisation which has as its basic aim the strengthening of the National Identity in a 32 County Ireland through the preservation and promotion of Gaelic Games and pastimes'.

But no matter what you put down on paper, the reality is that playing gaelic games in the northern six of those 32 counties has always been a bit different to the rest of the country.

The differences could be the biggest thing imaginable – being killed for being a member of the GAA. To the most trivial – being patted on the head and told to, 'Keep the game going up there'.

And with everything in between.

I WAS BORN in 1962, so when The Troubles began at the end of the decade I was old enough to have some idea of what was going on. But because my experience was from the television, it didn't seem quite real.

Cloughmills was a quiet place in the country – though like everywhere in the north The Troubles would visit here too; the police station was blown up in a massive bomb attack. Then, on the television, you were seeing armoured cars and explosions on the streets of Derry and Belfast, people being killed, and rows of houses being burned to the ground.

I saw all this going on and I wondered if it could come to Cloughmills? As far as I could tell, this stuff on the TV looked like a Western you might see on another channel. You could get a crowd of boys who might get on a bus and be in Cloughmills an hour later, bringing all the mayhem on the screen with them.

Like a posse of cowboys riding into town! I didn't know any better, but how is any child supposed to make sense of something like that?

I remember going to a match up in Belfast when I was young. We were coming from the pitch in the west of the city and were driving through the city centre when, all of a sudden, my dad stopped the car and headed in a different direction. He obviously saw something we were oblivious too; trouble he wanted to keep us from to get us home safely.

Thank God, I never lost anybody in the family through The Troubles. So many families weren't so lucky.

Frank Corr was the father of Jim, who I took over from as the county goalkeeper. Frank was from the Ardoyne club in north Belfast and was the secretary of the South Antrim Divisional Board. He was involved with my dad in the management of the county team at the start of the 70s. He was great mates with my dad and, like him, lived and breathed hurling.

Antrim were playing Galway in the 1972 All-Ireland quarter-final in Ballycastle and, right in the middle of the bloodiest year in the history of The Troubles, the Galway team were nervous about heading north. So, Frank travelled down to Monaghan to meet the bus before getting on to guide them along safe roads all the way up to Ballycastle.

After the match, he escorted them back down, before driving back home to Belfast. He went 400 miles out of his way to make sure Galway could get to Ballycastle and back to safely play a game of hurling.

Less than a week later, Frank went out to work and never came home. Loyalist paramilitaries had kidnapped him, beaten him and shot him dead. Frank's body was found in his burning car, along with another victim of his killers. My dad never spoke about it – he wasn't that sort of person, but I know that affected him. How could it not?

WE HAD TO move out of the house ourselves for a time as well. In his work as a building contractor, my dad had done a lot of work for a farmer outside the village, building sheds and that sort of thing. One night, the farmer was sitting in a bar in Clough, not far from Cloughmills, having a drink when he overheard three men sitting at a table, planning my dad's assassination. The farmer let my dad and the police know, and we had to move out until the threat had passed.

Even after we were back in the house, I was worried about him. After that, when I'd be with him and he was on his sales visits in bars and the like, I would start to worry. If I thought he was taking longer than normal, I would start to panic a bit, worried that he might have been kidnapped. He always came back out and I never said a word to him, but I couldn't help it. I was in my early teens and was worried about my dad.

The same thing crossed my mind when he was up in Belfast for GAA meetings. It's 40 miles from Belfast to Cloughmills and travelling those roads late at night in the 70s could make anyone nervous, never mind someone waiting at home for them.

But my dad just bore on and never let it bother him. He wasn't going to change the way he was. He'd sit in Gilly McIlhatton's house and chat for hours, not worried that he might not get back to Cloughmills until two or three in the morning. And when he was doing the sales in the pubs, he'd have the job done in about 15 minutes but then sit with a cup of tea and just chat away, as time went by.

He couldn't turn down a cup of tea and a chat. Plenty of times when I'd be out in the car with him it would be nine o'clock at night before we'd get back, when it could just have easily been three or four hours earlier.

I always wondered what must have been going through mammy's head in a time before mobile phones, and not knowing when he was coming back. Years later, I asked if she was worried when my dad would be up in Belfast for a meeting and wouldn't get back until the early hours, especially when things were at their worst in the city. She said it wasn't something she thought about. She knew what he was like, that he'd be sitting talking hurling, and he'd be back when he was back. And he always was.

As much as my dad – and everyone – tried to get on with things, I'm sure there were scary times as well. He told me about coming back from Belfast from a meeting one night and as they came over the Black Mountain, one of the fellas in the car said, 'The city's in darkness there, stop the car… and we'll see what's going on!'

They pulled over to the side of the road and got out of the car to look down on the city and see what was happening. All of a sudden, they heard a whirring noise and from out of nowhere an army armoured car came flying down the road. But for the noise, they would have had no idea this thing was coming at them, out of the darkness. My dad had to be pulled out of the way or he would have been hit.

ABOUT A YEAR after the Patrick Og's team was formed in Cloughmills, windows of Catholic homes and the parochial house in the village were smashed. The police suspected 'Sabbatarians' who weren't happy that the team were going to be playing Loughgiel in a match on a Sunday.

But the fact that after a year of only playing away matches this was going to be the first one at home, and that a grave was dug on the pitch with a cross bearing the name of the local priest, made it clear they didn't want any matches to be played at all. It's no wonder the club didn't last long.

The Cloughmills I grew up in genuinely felt very different. I used to practice my hurling at the end of the house, where the shop wall was, and my Protestant friends would come out and play with me, taking shots at me in goals. I played football along with these guys and they were just big into sport, whatever it was. It wasn't a case then that they'd say… 'I'm not going to play that, that's a Catholic game!'

Cloughmills was always a mainly Unionist village and Union Jacks would fly on lamp posts over where we were playing hurling. I was just used to it. It was of great interest to some of the reporters who appeared around the time Antrim were in the All-Ireland final. It made for a great picture in the Dublin papers, but I thought nothing of it. In all my time playing under those flags, since I was a youngster, there was no animosity – it didn't come into it.

Police would come along and try to take the sticks or the ball off us, but that stopped when we were big enough to look after ourselves. They'd say we couldn't play on the road. I'd ask why? And they'd tell me I could damage someone's car.

I told them that if I damaged someone's car, I'd pay for it. It got to the stage that they knew we wouldn't be pushed around anymore and they left us alone. But that wasn't just hurling, it was the same when we played football. They just came around acting the big men until they knew we would stand up to them.

One of my best friends was very high up in the Orange Order. He worked in the Michelin tyre plant in Ballymena and when Antrim got the All-Ireland final, he took the Sunday off to watch the match on TV. He would have known 'Cloot' as well through soccer. He very nearly lost his job over the head of it. He knew he couldn't give them the real reason he was taking the day off, so he gave them an excuse and then they found out he was watching the hurling.

Another Protestant friend I played soccer with asked me if there was any chance I could get him a ticket for the final. That's what the tickets are for – to give to family and give to friends. He went down to Croke Park and loved it.

MUSIC TOOK ME places you'd never expect to find an Antrim hurler. Rangers supporters clubs in places like Carrickfergus and Larne, and local football clubs in staunchly Unionist areas, were good gigs to get and I never had any bother at any of them.

I was playing with the Kathy Kane Band in the Carrick Rangers club one night and there was a fella who managed the club called Raymond Hill, a big gentleman, and when you came in to set up the gear you went in to the office to see him. Normally it would just be a matter of popping in to tell Raymond everything was ready, and then he'd go down and introduce the band.

We'd all find our spots. Raymond would come up on stage as the drummer would be counting in and he'd say, 'Ladies and gentlemen, please put your hands together for the Kathy Kane Band!' BANG… away you'd go.

On this particular night, I went in to see Raymond to tell him we were ready and he said to me, 'I didn't know you played hurling.'

'To be honest, Raymond, I was trying to keep it quiet.'

'Sure, it's not a bit of bother, we love the game in here. There was a match that came on the other night and someone said, "Jesus, that's big Niall!" and we sat and watched it. You'll get no bother in here, we're delighted to have you.'

So, he goes up on stage, the drummer starts counting in, and Raymond announces…

'Ladies and gentlemen, please put your hands together for…'

I was expecting him to say… 'The Kathy Kane Band'.

But Raymond said… 'The big hurler from Loughgiel!' Our drummer stopped mid-count, sticks in the air… terrified.

At another club on the Shankill Road in Belfast, we were treated like lords. They carried the gear in and out of the van and laid on all the tea and sandwiches you could want. As nice as ninepence. That was on a Saturday night. Sitting at home on Monday watching the news, I saw somewhere that looked very familiar. The police had raided the club and found a bomb factory in one of the rooms.

We only played that place once.

While we never had any trouble, because of the times the way they were in the early-80s, I was trying to keep a low profile when I was playing places like that. We were playing Galway in an All-Ireland quarter-final, but the night before I was playing the Harland & Wolff club in east Belfast.

The barman came up to me and asked, 'Is that your photo on the back page of *Ireland's Saturday Night?*'

'I don't know, I haven't seen it.'

So, he brought me the sports paper that used to be published in the north and there I was.

'There's a man down there wants to talk to you.'

Well, that had me on my nerves right away. I didn't know what was going to happen.

It was George Best's father Dickie.

He wanted to talk to me because he was fascinated by hurling. I sat down and started chatting to him, and tried to explain it as best as I could and answer his questions. It was a thrill for me because George Best was the reason I was a Man United supporter.

And his father was just a lovely wee man.

I PLAYED IN all sorts of places, for all sorts of people, and the only gig I didn't play was when I was about 18. A fella rang to see if we'd do a gig in Derry – although the ones who wanted us to play for them wouldn't have called it that.

We were offered the gig and the money was three times what we were getting anywhere else. That was great and we landed up in Derry, but couldn't get parked at the door of the place; we had to park about six car lengths up. Me and the driver went in to check the place out and see how we'd get the gear in, that sort of thing.

'Are you the band?'

'We are.'

'Upstairs!'

So, we went upstairs and there must have been 500 people in the room. It was full of soldiers, with a marching band in the middle of everything playing all the Loyalist tunes.

We went back down the stairs and said to the fella at the door that we were just going to get in the van, go round the block and see if we could find a spot closer to the door… handier for moving in our gear. We got back into the van and headed straight back down the road home. I was looking over my shoulder the whole way, and I don't think I relaxed until I was about an hour away and could see Ballymoney.

I got a phone call the next day.

'What happened yous last night? I'll tell you this… you'll never play for me again!'

I didn't argue. I don't think I've ever been so scared in my life.

THE SAME DAY we beat Dublin to get promoted to Division One for the first time, the SAS shot dead three members of the IRA in Gibraltar. That was the start of one of the most infamous sequences of events in the history of The Troubles. At the funerals a week and a half later, a Loyalist launched an attack that killed three of the mourners. Then, at one of their funerals, two British Army soldiers drove into the procession right outside Casement Park, were dragged out of their car, and later shot dead by the IRA.

That was the day before we were supposed to play Tipperary in the National League quarter-final.

The days between our match against Dublin and the Tipp match were some of tensest the north had ever seen, and we couldn't escape it either.

Normally, we'd have been training in Belfast, but it just wasn't possible. It was decided to keep the training in the north of the county because it was safer. Most of the panel were from north Antrim and having car-loads of hurlers coming into Belfast at that time wouldn't have been safe – it was simple as that.

When we headed down to the Tipp match, the road to Dublin was still lined with black flags that had been put up in mourning for the bodies of the three IRA members killed in Gibraltar a fortnight earlier.

At other times, when boys who worked in Belfast were being collected from work for training, Jim Nelson or Sean McGuinness would tell them – under no circumstances be waiting with a hurling stick. You just couldn't take the risk.

Around the same time that year we were coming home from training one night at the Antrim Forum complex that had pitches and a running track. Jim told us what drills we were working on and what the tactics would be, but the most important thing we had to be sure of was genuinely scary. No other team preparing for the All-Ireland Hurling Championship had to take the precautions we did.

Every night, before we went out, Jim made it clear:

'We have this place to ourselves tonight, lads. If you see any car headlights coming into that car park, don't think... just run. Get into the dark as quickly as you can!'

That's how bad things were.

We were coming home from training there one night with myself, 'Cloot' and I think 'Woody', Sean Paul and Declan McKillop in the car. We came up over the mountain and there was a UDR – a local British Army regiment – checkpoint. We were pulled in and there were maybe six cars coming the other way... queued up on the road.

We were stopped and the UDR men opened the boot to see the hurling sticks.

'Right, stand over there at the ditch, boys!'

The next thing, all the cars heading the other direction were waved through. It was just us and them. *This doesn't look good,* I thought to myself. There was either going to be a shooting-match here or they were going to plant something to get us into bother. I thought we were in real trouble.

We were lined up and one of the UDR boys was being especially ignorant, in our faces, while another one of them started going through our bags in the boot of the car. In one of the bags there was a programme from an old match, I can't remember which one... but 'Cloot' was on the front of it.

The UDR man came over to 'Cloot'.

'Is that you on the cover of that programme?'

'It is, aye.'

'Are you the boy that played for Armoy against Glentoran in the Irish Cup?'

'I am!'

'Cloot' had played sweeper when the Armoy United soccer team had made it to the fourth round of the Irish Cup, a great achievement for a wee club like that. They went up to play Glentoran, who had won the cup four years in-a-row, at the

Oval in east Belfast, and even though they lost 5-1 the Glentoran supporters gave them a standing ovation as they left the pitch.

'Can I keep that programme?' said the UDR man. 'And could you sign it for me? I'm a Glentoran supporter and was at the Oval that day.'

But for that programme and 'Cloot' being on the front of it, I don't know what would have happened.

'Right boys, get into the car… off yous go!'

NOT EVERY DIFFERENCE or difficulty for GAA people in the north was a matter of life and death, and not every difference or difficulty was because of non-GAA people. Attitudes from supporters, players, managers and administrators – sometimes unintentional, sometimes not – couldn't help but make you feel you were an outsider, even in your own association.

Justin McCarthy wrote in his book about how he was shocked, when he was working with my dad and the Antrim team for the 1970 Intermediate Championship, that when they went down to play Galway the home supporters were calling the players… 'Orangemen'.

It's something teams from the six counties have always had to deal with and every so often you'll hear stories of players getting targeted by that sort of ignorant stuff. Thankfully, I didn't experience much of it in my career, but it did happen, and when you heard it, you could get annoyed, though it says far more about the people giving out the abuse than it did us.

One time, I do remember us getting stick down in Carlow at an important Division Two match. It'll go down as a big day in Antrim hurling history, as that was the day 'Sambo' made his county debut. There were steps going up to the changing rooms and 'Hippy' slipped on them, fell and hurt his back. As a result, 'Sambo' came in and played for Antrim for the first time. I wasn't playing myself that day which meant I got a front row seat to the sort of abuse that I thankfully didn't get to hear too often in my years playing.

At Dr Cullen Park, there's long tunnel to get to the pitch and I came out of it with Ger Rogan, who was also a sub that day, and went over to take a seat on the bench. As soon as the team came out a pair of old women, hanging over the fence and waving their umbrellas, started right behind us.

'Get away back up to the black north you orange…'

'Rogie', from the heart of west Belfast, wasn't going to sit and listen to that. He stood up, turned round and drove his stick into the wire fence. They weren't long in stepping back and shutting up. There wasn't another peep out of them all afternoon.

It wasn't just supporters. During the 1987 All-Ireland semi-final against Kilkenny in Dundalk we were called every name in the book by some Kilkenny players. It was unreal and something I had never experienced. Maybe I was a little removed from it because I was in goals, not marking anybody, so never had to put up with an opponent in my ear.

I know Brian Donnelly for one wasn't left alone for the entire match.

'You orange this... You black that.'

Everything. Just horrible stuff – the last thing you'd expect on a hurling pitch.

THANKFULLY, I FOUND that sort of thing a rare occurrence. When it happened, you were a bit taken back by it but you could not let it annoy you because it didn't happen too often and you could dismiss it as nasty ignorance.

The gentler, but more constant, thing you had to put up with was training just as hard as any team in the country... giving up just as much, and a lot of the time hurling just as well as any other team... and then being patted on the head for it! Instead of being genuinely respected.

We wanted to earn our place against the top teams and then be treated like everyone else. It was up to us to get to that level, and we kept working at it, but no matter what we did, we'd be patronised again and *again*.

We weren't alone in that. The way hurling is, with its three aristocrats and a few established counties, means that anyone else below that level can find themselves treated that way. Offaly and Galway struggled for years the same way we did, before they made their breakthroughs in the 80s and then kicked on to great success. They had found themselves looked down on like we were because they weren't Cork or Kilkenny or Tipperary. *They shouldn't be there.* I don't think it's any coincidence that we always found Offaly and Galway – as both teams and counties – the most respectful and helpful to us as we were trying to emulate what they had achieved. They knew what it was like.

If I heard, 'You're doing a great job, keep the game alive up there!' once... I heard it a hundred times.

I promised myself when we did finally beat a big team in a big match, I'd go into the other dressing-room and tell them, 'You're doing a great job, keep the game alive down there!' When it finally happened in 1989, the Offaly boys were waiting in a guard of honour to clap us off the pitch.

They could walk that line between being respectful and patronising.

Others didn't even try.

PART **FOUR**

'You're in... and you better do the business, boy!'

The hard years paid off when we defeated Offaly in the 1989 All-Ireland semi-final, but it was a victory that we had to literally spill blood for on the day in Croke Park.

My weight had crept back up on me once again by the time of that historic year in 1989 and, in hindsight, it did hinder my performance.

We had Jim Nelson (left) to thank for bringing us to the All-Ireland final against Tipperary in 1989. Great men had come before him and they did their part, but Jim's brilliant management offered us the finishing touch as a team. We were a band of brothers (below) by the time that brilliant year came around, and we also had so many good people around us to make sure that Antrim could compete against the best in the country. Men like Dr Alasdair McDonnell and county chairman Oliver Kelly, seen here lifting Jim on high.

« CHAPTER 8 »

MY DAD RETIRED as manager before the 1984-'85 season, but he didn't step away completely. He stayed on as a selector – Kevin Donnelly was back on board as well, with Sean McGuinness in as the manager. Sean, who passed away in 2021, was as good a motivator as I ever played for and he played a big part in moving Antrim forward some of the steps to get us to where we wanted to be.

In my opinion, he wouldn't have been as tactically aware as someone like Jim Nelson – though some other players might tell you different – but he was a very good manager and a fantastic motivator, as he also showed with Down when he helped them make their breakthrough in 1992. If you had one good thing in your game, Sean would get it out of you. We had been slowly building for years but Sean was the first man who really put the belief into players that we could get into Division One and get into an All-Ireland final.

He wasn't one for rigid plans of how to play, but we enjoyed that too because it gave us a wee bit of freedom to express ourselves. Getting the most out of the team and winning were what mattered, and it didn't matter to Sean how we did it.

He also gave a wee bit of leeway as far as drinking was concerned. Sean treated us like adults and trusted that if we went for a pint the night before a game, we'd have just that – a pint, not 10.

There was one night his trust was a bit misplaced.

The year after the Centenary Cup, the GAA held an Open Draw Cup and we had to go down to play Laois in Borris-in-Ossory. Laois were an established Division One side, had reached the Centenary Cup final the year before and we weren't expecting to trouble them. Because I was playing with the band on the Saturday night, I didn't travel down with the team, and so I didn't arrive at the hotel until maybe four o'clock on the Sunday morning. When I got there, there were about half a dozen of the boys running about steaming. It was some scene.

I found out my room number and went up to bed. My room-mate wasn't tucked up. He was one of the wide-awake boys and, when I got into the room, he was on the phone to the night porter looking for more drink. The night porter politely declined. That didn't go down well.

McGuinness got wind of what had gone on – to be fair, it was hard to miss – and at breakfast he cracked up and read the riot act. But he wasn't going to give the boys 'suffering' the afternoon off and he started with the same team that was originally picked. Two of the boys who had been airlocked a few hours earlier lasted about 10 minutes, but we scored four goals in the first 20 minutes and ended up beating them by two points. In the next round, we pushed Tipp to four points in Thurles and we were in a good place heading into the championship.

That maybe surprised some people, as we only avoided being relegated from Division Two by the skin of our teeth. We lost to Kerry in our last match but stayed up because Clare beat Waterford on the same day.

We were nearly surprised ourselves when we played London in the All-Ireland quarter-final at Casement. They were winning by a point at half-time and went further ahead at the start of the second-half. Dessie Donnelly got his second goal, but London kept coming at us and with five minutes left looked just as likely winners as us, with the scores level. Thank God for Dessie, who scored the last three points.

If the London match was a bit too exciting as far as we were concerned, the semi-final against Offaly was nearly the exact opposite. It was played in one of the least likely All-Ireland hurling semi-final venues ever – the Athletic Grounds in Armagh – and the rain didn't stop for a second. We were on a heavy football pitch and it obviously took Offaly some time to get used to it.

We got the first three points and Collie Donnelly maybe could have had a goal before Offaly scored but, soon enough, they found their feet and after they scored two goals in the space of three minutes, we were chasing the game. We had more goal chances of our own, but couldn't take them.

That lifted the pressure from them – and there was always pressure on the big southern teams when they played us because nobody expected them to lose – and by half-time they were 11 points ahead. We kept going in the second-half and they only beat us by point after the break.

It was by far the closest we'd got to beating a team like Offaly in the championship.

And they went on to win the All-Ireland that year. It was definitely another step forward.

THAT 1985-'86 LEAGUE was Antrim's best for years. We drew with Wexford at Casement on the first day – and that ended up the only point Wexford dropped.

Dessie Donnelly was in unbelievable form. He seemed to be scoring two or three goals in every match and he ended up the top scorer in the entire National League that season. Against Wexford, he scored a goal from a free about 40 yards out with seven men on the line, to get us a draw. With two matches left we were right in the hunt for promotion, but went down to Kerry and were hammered. Even after that, we knew if we could beat Westmeath in Mullingar, we'd be promoted to Division One.

Just like Kerry, we had some really tough battles with Westmeath.

Some of our matches were bloodbaths. Brian Donnelly had his appendix out but came back for the Westmeath match. Not long into the game Brian got a dig in the stomach… and that was him taken out of commission. Down the other end, David Kilcoyne gave us a torrid time. He ended up winning an All Star that year – we just couldn't get a hold of him. We lost by five points and had to watch as Westmeath were promoted.

With the championship round the corner, I had a big decision to make. The music was as busy as it had ever been. We could hardly keep up with the bookings and I knew things weren't going to get any quieter as we headed into the summer.

So, at training in Waterfoot one night, I told Sean that I was going to pull out of the panel. Sean asked me what was wrong and I told him my reasons. I just wouldn't have time to get to training and I said you can't expect Paul Smith, who was the sub goalkeeper, to be sitting on the bench having trained every night. I was only there once a week, maybe once a fortnight.

Sean told me he'd prefer me to stay, but I was adamant – it wouldn't have been fair to Paul. Looking back, I'm sure Sean probably would have let me stay on the panel as a reserve goalkeeper to Paul, but I didn't push it. Though that wouldn't have been fair to whoever I would be keeping off the bench either.

Shortly after that, I was playing up in the Sarsfield's club in Belfast – which was Sean's club. People could send up requests on a bit of paper I had one passed to me and I opened it… and it just read… 'To the man who sold his soul'.

Jesus, I thought. That hurt me.

I don't know who sent it up but they obviously thought I had turned my back on my county. But I hadn't turned my back; I just didn't think it was fair to Paul Smith or anyone else when I couldn't give the commitment they were giving.

Even though we had showed we had improved against Offaly the year before and were one match away from being a Division One team in the league, everyone expected Cork would do exactly the same to Antrim in the 1986 All-Ireland semi-final as they had in 1984.

It didn't help that I wasn't the only regular missing. Seven of us who played against Westmeath didn't play against Cork for one reason or another. Sean McNaughton was the captain and full-back, but he was suspended for three months after getting sent off in a club game. Tony McGrath was brilliant against Joachim Kelly in the semi-final the year before but he was working in England. 'Sambo' had been over in America. No one saw what eventually happened coming. The next day in the papers, Sean McGuinness said it was the best ever performance from an Antrim hurling team. It was hard to argue with him.

Antrim got 25 scores to Cork's 18… but seven of Cork's were goals compared to only one for Antrim. They scored 17 points in the first-half but Cork's goals meant they were leading by three at half-time.

I was sitting in the house, listening to the game on the radio. At half-time I left the house and went up to the chapel to say a prayer that Antrim would win. As I listened to the rest of the match, I had tears in my eyes because I was listening to commentators talking about Antrim playing in Croke Park – and maybe even reaching an All-Ireland final – and I wasn't involved.

It was the first championship match I had missed since I joined the senior panel nearly seven years earlier. In the end, Cork won by four points but had been given an almighty scare. My prayer for an Antrim win hadn't been answered but it made me think what it would have been like for Antrim to win an All-Ireland semi-final… and me not to be part of it. I wasn't going to give up on the chance of playing for my county again.

If Antrim were going to get to an All-Ireland final, I was determined to be there with them.

JIM NELSON IS Antrim's most successful manager ever, but he was an *accidental* manager. 1986 had been Antrim's best season in years. Even though there was the disappointment of just missing out on promotion, the All-Ireland semi-final against Cork had caused a stir. So, when the league started that autumn there was some expectation about the team.

The first couple of matches were the toughest – against Tipperary and Waterford – and we lost both of them but that wasn't the reason that, the week before their third match against Meath, Sean McGuinness quit as manager. There was an internal row in Sarsfield's, and Sean wasn't happy with how the thing was dealt with in the county, so he stepped down.

Antrim needed a manager and, as it turned out, the perfect man was already head of the hurling board. Jim Nelson came in to replace Sean on a temporary basis and Antrim beat Meath… then Kerry and Mayo in their last three league matches before the end of the year. When the county convention came around, Jim was made the permanent manager.

All this was happening while I was still off the panel. After Jim was ratified as the manager, he came to me and asked if I'd come back on board for the second part of the league after Christmas. By that stage Sean McNaughton's suspension was over, so the two of us returned to the panel for the last two matches in Division Two.

We were still in the hunt for promotion but needed to beat Laois and Dublin, and hope someone did us a favour by taking points off Tipp or Waterford, who had beaten us before Christmas. We never got the favour, but couldn't beat Laois anyway, and my first match back was on the bench when we drew at Casement.

Our last match was against Dublin in Croke Park. And with the result not meaning anything – drawing against Laois meant we couldn't be promoted, but our pre-Christmas wins meant we couldn't be relegated either – Jim gave the subs a run out. I played my first match for the county in nearly a year.

It was good to be back – and good to win as well – but I knew Paul was the man with the No 1 jersey and I'd have to take it off him… if I wanted it.

That year we had an All-Ireland quarter-final to play against the 'B' champions, who were our old foes London, and in the lead-up to that we played challenge matches with Paul in the nets for one game and me for the next.

Jim picked Paul for the London match and we beat them by five points at Casement to qualify for an All-Ireland semi-final against the Leinster champions.

Our last challenge match before that was down in Ballinasloe against Galway. I played, and when it came to pick the team, I got the nod.

Fergus McNaughton, one of the selectors came in and told me, 'You're in… and you better do the business, boy!'

'Why's that?'

'I'm just after getting pinned against the wall there by big Kevin, because you're in instead of Paul.'

Kevin Donnelly was still one of the selectors and he obviously wasn't happy that Paul had been dropped. I don't hold anything against Kevin for that. Paul was his clubmate and he hurled in front of him for years as the Ballycastle full-back. I was behind Kevin one year with the county and he obviously thought Paul was the better choice, which he was quite entitled to do. I never realised how good a full-back Kevin was until I played behind him – and I'd still have a good chat with Kevin when I meet him.

As far as I was concerned, I had come back when I was asked, trained and played, done my best, and the selectors decided to pick me. I hadn't been complaining or expecting to play. I came back and sat on the bench when I was asked to, and played when I was asked to.

Paul Smith's reaction told me everything I needed to know about him. After the team was picked he came up to me. 'Niall, I'm really annoyed I'm not playing and I'll not be stripping out. It's nothing against you… but I'm not happy, and that's me.'

We shook hands and he wished me all the best.

And that's what Paul is like… a great, *great* fella.

IF ARMAGH, TWO years before, was a strange place for an All-Ireland semi-final then Dundalk in 1987 managed to at least match it.

Part of the reason we were there was Bono and his mates. U2 played two concerts at Croke Park at the end of June and the pitch was left in a complete *state*. That meant the Leinster final between Kilkenny and Offaly had to be pushed back a week.

The knock-on was that our semi-final had to be delayed as well to give Kilkenny, who beat Offaly by a goal, a week off before they played us. Croke Park was ruled out as a venue because Galway and Cork were playing a football semi-final there the same day.

The first option, and one Antrim were right behind, was to toss for the venue and play in either Casement or Nowlan Park. Kilkenny weren't interested. Even a 50/50 chance of having to come to Casement was too much for them.

Jim said his piece in the papers about how playing the match in Dundalk at the same time the football semi-final was on TV showed the GAA didn't care about promoting hurling, but behind closed doors we thought Kilkenny refusing to toss for the venue showed that they were worried. It was actually a sign of respect.

Those big southern teams never liked coming up to the north to play us and after Kilkenny saw what nearly happened to Cork the year before, they obviously didn't want to take the chance.

It wasn't just Kilkenny who had obviously taken note of the Cork match the year before. That day in Dundalk was the first time the Antrim supporters really came out in force for us. Whenever we arrived at the ground and headed into the dressing-room about an hour before the match there were a couple of buses there, but when we came out the place was absolutely stuffed. People hanging over the wire, sitting on walls… they were *everywhere,* and they all seemed to be from Antrim.

I think having all those supporters behind us lifted our game and we flew into Kilkenny. We scored 1-5 before they even got on the board, and were the better team all over the field. Dessie Donnelly was knocking over frees and Danny McNaughton flicked in a brilliant overhead goal.

Kilkenny got into the match after that but we were still winning by five points at half-time.

We were against the breeze in the second-half but had shown that we could match Kilkenny. Harry Ryan got a goal back for them right at the start of the second-half but we were at a point now where that sort of setback wouldn't make us buckle. Danny doubled another high ball into the net... and we were five points up.

At this stage, we were going score-for-score and five minutes after Danny got his second goal the Kilkenny corner-forward Liam McCarthy got a ball and ran across the square. I came out and didn't even tackle him.

He ran straight into me and took a lot of steps doing it.

Penalty!

Ger Fennelly took it and I stopped it... but didn't kill it. I threw myself out at it, to try and get the rebound, but Harry Ryan got to it before me and buried it. We were still ahead until about 20 minutes from the end, when Kilkenny got level for the first time. We got a point, they got a point... we got a point... they got a point!

With six minutes left, we were level.

Antrim hadn't been this close to an All-Ireland final in more than 40 years. But the effort it had taken us to get there started to tell, and so did Kilkenny's experience. In those last six minutes they scored seven points, and we couldn't manage one. They knocked over their frees – some of them a result of 'tired tackling' but a lot from the sort of tackles that would never be a foul in an Antrim club match, or even the other All-Ireland semi-final between Galway and Tipperary.

Long before Jim was the manager, we had problems with refereeing.

We felt we were getting a rough deal and the coaches had tried to sit down with referees to get things clear about what was a foul and what wasn't. But no matter how many meetings and how many clarifications there were, it felt that when we went down south, we had to play by different rules.

Sometimes, you got the feeling the referee was ready for us, ready to blow for a foul before it even happened because it was Antrim, and they were expecting something. But we could complain all we wanted. We had lost again and that's all that mattered. But in our first year under Jim, we had shown that we weren't going away. We deserved our place in the All-Ireland semi-final.

Now we wanted to earn our place in Division One.

WE HAD FIVE league matches to play before Christmas, and Jim had us convinced we could win every one of them. In the end we won three – Offaly beat us at Casement and Kerry won in Killarney – against Roscommon, Westmeath and Down, who were up in Division Two for the first time in years. That was a tight, tough match – and a sign of things to come.

Our two matches in the new year would decide promotion. Offaly had beaten everyone and were clear at the top, but second place was up for grabs between ourselves, Laois and Dublin – with The Dubs in the driving seat. If they won their last two matches, against Kerry and us, they'd go up.

We needed a favour and we got it the day we beat Laois, as Kerry beat Dublin with a last-minute goal. That meant our match against Dublin at Casement was winner-takes-all. The papers called it the biggest hurling match played in Antrim since the 1943 All-Ireland semi-final when Kilkenny came up and lost. The supporters obviously believed the papers because the stand at Casement was packed that Sunday.

For the full hour, the noise never stopped and, thankfully, we were giving them something to shout about. We started with the wind and made the most of it, thanks as well to a couple of mistakes from the Dublin goalkeeper. First, he fumbled a ball in from Brian Donnelly that 'Cloot' flicked into the net. Then a few minutes later, Ger Rogan lobbed a ball in from the sideline that dropped in front of the 'keeper… and went through his legs.

We were 11 up at half-time, and when 'Beaver' put us 12 up at the start of the second-half we had one foot in Division One. Then I made a mistake when I came out but couldn't take a high ball, and they scrambled it over the line. They got another goal soon after and, all of a sudden, our lead was down to three.

But the crowd kept going and, I think, kept us *going*. Paul McKillen – 'Humpy' – was brilliant in midfield and our defence made sure they didn't get the goal they needed. When the final whistle went, we were four points up and heading for Division One for the first time ever.

As far as we were concerned, that was job done, but getting promoted meant we had a league quarter-final to play against Tipp. Not for the first time – and definitely not for the last time – Nicky English destroyed us. We were hardly alone in that back then – he was just unstoppable. He scored a couple of goals in the first-half as they beat us by 11 points.

Over the past couple of years Antrim had given Cork and Kilkenny their fill of it in All-Ireland semi-finals. Now we had to try and do the same to hurling's other great aristocrat – Tipperary.

After they beat us in the quarter-final they had gone on to win the league and then easily retained their Munster title. So, even though Antrim had come close to upsetting the odds the previous two years, they were red hot favourites to beat us in the All-Ireland semi-final.

'Cloot' nearly had the ball in the net right from the throw-in when he just missed flicking in a ball from Brian Donnelly, but that wasn't a flash in the pan. We went toe-to-toe with them all through the first-half.

English was fouled for a penalty that Pat Fox scored, but almost straightaway 'Cloot' got his goal at the other end. Fergus McAllister got another one and 'Humpy' and Ciaran Barr were giving Tipp all sorts of problems. But Tipp were always doing enough to keep ahead of us and English got his usual goal right after Fergus got his, and they were two points up at half-time.

They pulled away a bit at the start of the second-half and probably finished us off when Ken Hogan made a brilliant save from Ciaran Barr, before Tipp came straight down the field and Fox ran in along the end-line and hand-passed past me for their third goal.

The match was effectively over, but there was still time for me to make it interesting… when I should have been sent off live on TV. Declan McKillop from our club wasn't long out of minor, making his championship debut for Antrim… and he was marking Pat Fox. That would have been tough enough as it was, but Fox was giving him a hard time… off the ball stuff! And I was seeing this, so when one ball came in and Fox came in after it, I caught it and buried him with my shoulder.

Hardly a fair contest, but I thought it needed to be done.

He ended up lying at my feet and I got a free out for him charging me, which was a nice change because being a big guy I didn't get as many frees as I think I should have for forwards coming in on me.

I scattered him and he told me what he thought of me and whatever else. I said to Declan, 'Declan, let him have it!' So, Declan started giving him a bit of lip too. Another ball came in and I put him down.

And I said to him, 'Is that all you've got?'

I never would have been like that; I always kept my mouth shut. If you were giving verbals… you weren't concentrating. But there was something different that day.

A ball came through and hit the side netting... wide. I bent down to lift the ball. Fox came through and drilled me across the wrist. So, I just swung and landed a right hook... right on the chin.

I heard a whistle.

I think I had looked to see who had hit me... and when I saw it was him, I just went... BANG! Maybe it was a snap reaction, I don't know. Maybe I saw him as he was coming in so I knew it was him.

But Pat Fox was lying there. I had hit him some dig.

The referee John Denton came in to me.

'RIGHT, YOU'RE AWAY!'

'John, I've never hit a man on the hurling field in my life.'

Which was a lie... *the Kerry game!*

I did everything to try to talk him out of sending me off. The photographer John 'Curly' McIlwaine swears he heard me saying... 'John, my dad's lying in bed sick and this would kill him!'

I don't believe that and I don't *remember* that, but 'Curly' swears I said that. I did everything but crawl up the referee's backside.

He said to me, 'Niall, if you as much as look at him... you're gone!'

And he booked me.

The boos started coming down on the field. Every time I touched the ball after that all you heard were the boos. I couldn't wait to get off. If you had asked me years later what happened at the final whistle, I'd have told you I just walked straight off the field to the dressing-room and didn't shake hands with anybody.

I just wanted *off*, I was so embarrassed.

But it turns out there was a picture in the paper the next morning of me shaking hands with Pat Fox – burst lip and all – on the pitch after the match. I'm glad I did shake his hand, because I wasn't proud of bursting him.

THAT WAS US out of the championship for another year, and the next night I got a phone call from Liam Currams, asking if I wanted to go out to New York and hurl for Offaly after the All-Ireland final.

'Aye. I wouldn't mind a trip out.'

Liam told me there was a fella, Frank Feary, who would call from America. Frank phoned me, introduced himself, asked if I was interested.

'Any man who puts the fear of God into the Tipperary forward line will do me!' he told me. I might not have been impressed with myself, by Frank obviously was.

'Who are we playing?' I asked.

'We're playing Tipperary in the semi-final of the championship!'

Of course, we were! And Tipp flew Pat Fox out to play for them!

So, out I went to play another championship semi-final against Tipperary, this time for Offaly and this time in Gaelic Park in The Bronx. The first ball of the match came in… a big high ball that I came out to meet, but Fox got to it before me.

I had no choice but to hit him with a shoulder.

'Not you again!'

After the game we shook hands and I apologised for hitting him. Whatever he might have thought of it, that was that as far as I was concerned.

We ended up losing. If we had won the semi-final they were going to fly me up to my aunt's in Canada to stay for the extra week, then fly me back down to play the final before heading home.

I stayed with a lovely older couple who looked after me and showed me around New York. That really opened up my eyes; it was a completely different world. That week in New York was a great experience and the following year when we were preparing for the All-Ireland final, the Offaly team I played for over there sent us over a cheque for the training fund.

Maybe a couple of years later, Kevin Cashman, who wrote for the *Examiner* down in Cork, came up to Loughgiel, as he did every year, to write stories about the hurling people in north Antrim. He loved the atmosphere up here, loved the hospitality in The Pound… and *loved* our *love* for hurling.

'When are you going to come forward Niall?'

'For what, Kevin?'

'For hurling for Offaly out in New York?'

'Not at all, Kevin.'

'Every dog in the street knows you were out, Niall.'

'Every dog in the street is WRONG, Kevin!'

He said that after the big furore over the 'Tony Keady Affair', when the legendary centre-back was suspended for a year for lining out in the Big Apple, the GAA wanted players to come forward and admit they had played illegally in

America. Anyone who did would be pardoned.

'Good for them, Kevin…. but's it's nothing to do with me!'

In the end, a lot of boys came forward and were suspended for their troubles. Thank God, I got away with it.

« CHAPTER 9 »

THE NIGHT BEFORE we played Offaly in the 1989 All-Ireland semi-final a reporter landed at the Grand Hotel in Malahide, where we were staying.

'Well, yous are here to do a good job?'

Jim Nelson didn't hesitate.

'We're here to win!'

'But realistically now, Jim, you'll be quite happy with running Offaly close, won't you?'

'We'll beat them!'

'I know you have to say that, Jim.'

'We'll be here tomorrow after the match. Come back and see us then.'

He never appeared.

We had a team meeting on the Saturday night before we went to bed and Michael O'Grady, who had coached with Tipp, Limerick and Wexford and was brought in by Jim to help us out, got up to speak. In no time, he had us champing at the bit.

The hair was standing on the back of my neck and every player left that room buzzing.

'Some people know you... a lot of people don't.

'Believe you me, come tomorrow night every one of you boys will be household names!'

OUR FIRST SEASON up in Division One couldn't have started any better. Wexford came up to Loughgiel and we beat them handy enough.

That meant we were top of Division One after the first Sunday of matches, but we lost our next five games... to Kilkenny, Waterford, Galway, Tipp and Limerick. Only an injury time save by Tommy Quaid from Collie Donnelly kept us from beating Limerick and we were close in the rest of the matches, except against Tipp down in Thurles, when I didn't play, as Jim gave Paul McStravick a run out in goals.

Another move Jim made that day was to start Dessie Donnelly at corner-back even though Dessie was one of the deadliest forwards in Antrim... or anywhere.

Jim tweaked things with the team a lot. He played boys in different positions and he must have played Dessie there in a challenge match or in training and saw something. Dessie was a wing-back when he came into the county team but he had been a corner-forward for years, and was the top scorer in the entire National League a few seasons before. I don't know if Jim thought Dessie was maybe starting to slow down a bit for corner-forward, but it was a great move.

He was a great player. As a corner-back he was so dogged. Wouldn't let you past him! A lot of people would say he was the best hurler amongst the Donnellys, but Brian's still my number one – probably because he broke my heart so often from under-12s up.

But Dessie was dynamite. If a forward gets a ball you've a fair idea from playing against these boys all the time what they're going to do, where they're going to aim their shot, if they're shaping for a goal or a point. Every time Dessie got a ball... he was going for goal. But just because you knew *what* he was going to do, that didn't mean you knew *how* he was going to do it.

You always had to be ready for the unexpected with Dessie.

One of the best saves I ever made was against Ballycastle in the championship. Dessie caught a ball about 18 yards out, maybe slightly closer. There was a ruck of players in front of me and he caught the ball, swivelled onto his left-hand side and drove it at the goal. I managed to catch the ball and clear it. Dessie's fist was in the air... he thought he'd scored the goal.

By 1991, he was back playing corner-forward with the county and scored a typical goal against Kilkenny in the All-Ireland semi-final. He got the ball, turned and buried it from a tight angle. He could hit a ball like a bullet.

The hardest shot I ever faced was from Randal McDonnell for Glenariffe. He hit a ball one time and I didn't see it until it bounced back out of the net over my shoulder. It was flying. Dessie would have been next on the list.

But, for the rest of 1989, Jim decided Dessie should be stationed at corner-back. He'd end up with an All Star.

AFTER ALL THE hard work we had put in to get up to Division One, we were staring, right in the face, the prospect of going straight back down after just one season.

We went into our last match knowing we'd have to beat Offaly to have any chance of staying up. Even if we did win, we'd still have to win some sort of play-off, either a one-off match against Offaly or as part of a three-way draw involving Wexford as well.

So, we headed down to Birr with our future in our hands.

We were missing Donal Armstrong and Ciaran Barr because Rossa were playing in the All-Ireland final a few days after the Offaly match. We could have done with everybody we had but Ciaran was an especially big loss, because not only was he our captain, but earlier that year he had been named as Antrim's first-ever All Star.

It was a cold, wet day down in Birr and, when we got there, there were a couple of old doors laid down in front of the posts to save the goalmouths because the pitch was such a mess.

We played into a gale in the first-half and got a couple of quick points, but then they took control and started knocking over scores. But they never pulled away as much as they should have done given how strong the breeze was. And we were only six points down at half-time... and still well in the game.

But the wind wasn't putting the ball over the bar for us and, in the conditions, it was a real slog to get anything going. Offaly only managed one point in the second-half and most of our scores were frees from 'Cloot', but they didn't look like being enough with time almost up. We were a point down and knew that a draw would be no good, so our only option was a goal.

With 30 seconds left, 'Sambo' sent a ball into 'Cloot' in the corner and he managed to somehow dip below his marker's arm and bury it to the net. It wouldn't be the last time that year 'Cloot' would manage the seemingly impossible against Offaly.

We had survived, but we weren't safe yet. Wexford had lost to Galway, which meant they finished on four points along with Offaly and ourselves, so a three-way play-off was needed to see who would be joining bottom placed Waterford in Division Two.

The first two teams drawn out of the hat would play each other, with the winner staying up and the loser playing the third team in a winner-takes-all match.

We were drawn out with Wexford, which was the best possible result for us as it meant we had two bites at safety. Offaly only had one chance, and that was what we wanted to avoid.

We had beaten Wexford by 10 points in the first match of the league in October, but it was a completely different story when we played them in the relegation play-off in Croke Park.

They blew us away!

It was the biggest beating we'd taken in a long time. They scored three goals in the first-half, and the only thing that goals from 'Sambo' and 'Woody' in the second did was take some of the bad look off the scoreboard. We still lost by 14 points.

Nothing they saw at Croke Park would have worried Offaly for the 'last chance saloon' play-off in Drogheda. But we were still confident, partly because we were a *confident* team, even when we were losing, and partly because we knew we had hardly hurled when we beat Offaly in Birr a couple of weeks earlier.

A lot of that was the weather and the pitch, but in Drogheda it was a lovely sunny day, so we knew there were no excuses. If we couldn't hurl there, we couldn't hurl anywhere.

It was a ding-dong battle from the first whistle, and we got off to a fast start. Ciaran Barr, who was back in the team and made a massive difference, was pulled down for a penalty that 'Beaver' put away, before Ciaran got the second goal himself. I made a decent save just before half-time and we were seven points ahead at the break.

Great crowds had followed us all that season and there were maybe five or six bus loads down in Drogheda. They were having a great Sunday afternoon in the sun and things got even better as the second-half got underway, and 'Cloot' and Donal Armstrong put us nine points ahead with about 25 minutes left.

A couple of quick Offaly goals later, and we were on the ropes.

The momentum had completely shifted and we couldn't stop them coming at us. We had gone from nine up to one down in less than 20 minutes. After those points at the start of the second-half we hadn't managed to score once and needed a point from 'Beaver' with three minutes left to force extra-time.

Ciaran Barr got another goal at the start of extra-time, but Offaly chipped their way back level. We went point-for-point until the end, but the strength of our panel saw us through when Mickey Sullivan and Sean Paul McKillop, who had both come off the bench, scored the last two points to keep us up.

The crowd celebrated like we'd won an All-Ireland – and it was an important match to win. Not only had we stayed in Division One, but we'd beaten Offaly for the second time that season, which would give us great confidence when we crossed paths with them again a few months down the line.

We didn't have much time to celebrate ourselves. After the game we had to get straight into our cars to go and play Rossa in an Antrim league match that night. We were absolutely knackered, but there was a full league programme for everyone.

I don't think many county players made much of an impact that evening.

EVEN THOUGH WE stayed up by the skin of our teeth, Jim viewed the league as a great success.

'The league is for learning… the championship is for winning!' he used to tell us.

Everything was geared towards the championship and the league was a springboard for that. Getting to a league quarter-final, as we had done the year before, was a bonus but it was an important one because it gave us another game to prepare for the championship when we needed as many top-class games as we could get. Our 1989 league had in some ways been even better because, even though they were relegation play-offs, we got two extra matches and we had saved our best performance for last.

What made another big difference was that the matches were in Division One for the first time. Each one brought us on a wee bit more. Before that, when we were playing in Division Two every year, we were just missing *something*… that little bit extra by the time we got to the championship, when something always let us down.

Geography was always part of our problem, and still is for Antrim teams trying to improve. You had to go at least as far as Dublin before you could get a decent challenge match where you were going to learn something.

Some southern teams would have come up to Dublin to meet us, but most of the time we'd have to travel further down for a weekend and then you'd need to play a match on a Saturday and a match on a Sunday to make it worth your while. Maybe a couple of matches in Galway or one in Tipperary… and then a stop in Offaly on the way back. But that took a lot of organisation and preparation and then there was the cost at a time when there wasn't a lot of money available to anyone, let alone the hurlers, who always felt we were treated as second-class citizens in Antrim.

OUR NINE DIVISION One matches were probably the best preparation before a championship season that an Antrim hurling team had ever had. We also played in the Oireachtas Cup competition for the first time, when Galway came up to Casement after the league was finished. We lost, but it was more important match practice. 'Cloot', who had scored a couple of goals over in New York where he played as an All Star replacement against Galway, carried his form back across the Atlantic and scored 1-8 against them at Casement. That boded well for us too.

The championship itself in 1989 would bring us more matches than usual because the Ulster Senior Championship, which hadn't been played since the 40s, was back on the calendar. Down had been improving over the past few years and had dominated the Ulster Under-21 Championship through the 80s. I was on the losing side in the 1983 final when Down football great Greg Blaney did the damage for their hurlers.

Down beat Derry in the semi-final and qualified to play us at the Athletic Grounds in Armagh for the Ulster title. We weren't troubled, but we weren't all that impressive either.

We took a while to get going and were only five points up at half-time. Like all matches against Down teams, no one took a step back on either side but when Danny McNaughton scored a couple of goals after half-time that killed the game, and we ended up easy winners. We'd have won by a lot more but for Down's brilliant goalkeeper Noel Keith.

It was good to get another game, and good to have things to work on in training. The same day we beat Down, Offaly surprised Kilkenny in the Leinster final, so we knew who'd we be up against in the All-Ireland semi-final. First, we had to get over Kildare, who had won the 'B' championship, in the quarter-final … on the same Dundalk pitch where we'd been so close to beating Kilkenny two years before.

The Kildare match wasn't anywhere near as exciting as the one against Kilkenny and we didn't play anywhere near as well. We scored three goals in the first-half but they were probably the better team; we just took our chances. We got better in the second-half and ended up winning by the guts of 20 points. But Jim wasn't happy with the performance – none of us were – and, worst of all, Danny McNaughton had gone off injured after getting a bang on the knee. It looked like he was going to miss the semi-final.

In other years that sort of thing might have thrown us off, or got into our heads. But we'd been on the road a long time and were going down to Dublin with one thought on our minds.

AFTER MICHAEL O'GRADY spoke to us in the hotel the night before the semi-final, we were ready to go straight to Croke Park, and break down the gates to get onto the field there and then. When we did get to Croke Park the next day, the place was heaving. Plenty of Antrim people were down for the match – but most of the crowd was made up of the people O'Grady talked about, who didn't know who we were.

We were well used to our All-Ireland semi-final being an afterthought. Since 1984, when Antrim were back at that stage of the championship against the Munster or Leinster champions, all the attention was always on the other match… the one Galway were playing in.

Against Offaly in 1985, and Kilkenny two years later, we were moved off to Armagh and Dundalk. 1988 was the first time they had a double-header in Croke Park and we were on first before the 'big match' between Galway and Offaly. In the end, Tipp only beat us by a point more than Galway beat Offaly.

But even though we were getting better and getting closer, the Antrim semi-final was still considered the warm-up act for the main event.

That would have been true in 1989 anyway, but the fact Galway were playing Tipperary in a repeat of the final from the year before, guaranteed it. And then there was 'The Keady Affair.'

The hurling headlines that summer were dominated by the news about Tony Keady, Galway's star centre-back. Keady was Hurler of the Year when Galway won their second All-Ireland in-a-row the previous season.

After Galway had beaten Tipp in the league final Keady went to New York on the All Stars trip but stayed on and played illegally for a club there.

When the GAA back home found out, he was slapped with that year-long ban, and a massive blow to Galway's hopes of a three in-a-row.

It was like a soap opera, with Galway threatening to withdraw from the championship and the GAA Management Committee voting narrowly to back Keady's suspension, which meant he wouldn't be playing against Tipp.

All the drama meant our match was even more of an afterthought than usual. It was all about Galway and Tipp… and everyone wanted to see it.

But that also meant that Croke Park, for probably the first time ever, was just about full to capacity for an All-Ireland semi-final.

Actually, two All-Ireland semi-finals. And almost everybody made it into the ground in time for our match with Offaly. Nearly 65,000 people – more than were at the final a year before. There weren't 3,000 people in Croke Park when we played Cork in the 1984 semi-final.

I doubt there were many in the 65,000 who thought the first semi-final would be anything other than a win for Offaly. But there was no doubt in our panel and our management that we could win – and it wasn't just Michael O'Grady's team talk.

PART **FIVE**

'Don't tell me Antrim beat Offaly?'

On the day of the 1989 final, we didn't do ourselves justice but we were also blown away by the brilliance of Nicky English (left), who also happened to be one of game's really good guys! And (below) after the 1988 semi-final, I congratulate Pat Fox and Donie O'Connell.

Our captain and inspirational leader Ciaran Barr (below) introduced us to the President of Ireland, Patrick Hillery before the game – another memory which will remain with me for life.

The Antrim team that took the field against Tipperary on that historic day in September 1989.

« CHAPTER 10 »

WE HAD PLAYED Offaly in two big matches already that season and, when it came to the biggest one of all, we knew exactly how we were going to go after them.

Ciaran Barr was named at full-forward but was going to be coming out to right half-forward, where he'd probably be marked by Ger Coughlan, who was a good half a foot shorter than Ciaran. After Michael O'Grady's team-talk, Ciaran spoke and told me, 'Pump balls down on top of me. I'll be over the top of him all day. Just keep them coming, Niall'.

In truth, I was spoiled for choice with that half-forward line because, as well as Ciaran coming out, you had 'Beaver', who had as good a hand as anyone I ever pucked a ball out to, and Brian Donnelly, who could catch *anything*. Jim told me to send the puckouts as far as I could every time.

If for some reason our half-forwards weren't winning it, then we could drop things shorter or bring the half-forward line on top of midfield – and then send the ball into the space between the full-forward line and the rest of the team. They could come out to meet it and feed the half-forward line coming through with hand-passes. That came off a few times in the match, but Plan A was to bombard our half-forwards.

Jim told us the ball we would win from that would win us the game. And it did.

Our physio Dan Turley had worked his magic on Danny McNaughton and he was fit enough to take his place on the bench for the semi-final. One of Jim

Nelson's biggest strengths was that he surrounded himself with the very best, and Dan was definitely that.

Dan was ahead of his time and introduced us to all sorts of things we'd never seen before from a physio. He brought sports science into it and we were well looked after. Dan would go on to work with the Armagh football team when they made their breakthrough at the end on the 90s before they won their All-Ireland.

With Danny in the subs, there was a bit of a reshuffle in the team. 'Sambo' was named at corner-forward and Dominic McMullan – who also needed Dan's help after he got injured in training the week before the match – coming in at midfield. Gary O'Kane, who was only 19 but earmarked for great things, had come on for Ger Rogan against Kildare and with 'Rogie' injured, Gary kept his place for the semi-final. Even though we had already beaten Offaly twice that year, even though we had a team full of experience of All-Ireland semi-finals, and even though we'd shown with every year that went past that we were getting a wee bit closer each time, we were still big underdogs for the match.

That suited us down to the ground.

If the papers had been talking us up as favourites it probably wouldn't have had an effect either, because the last thing an Antrim team could do back then, no matter how confident we were in ourselves, was to get complacent – especially when we were playing a team like Offaly.

Offaly might have respected us and our ability more than the likes of Cork, Kilkenny or Tipp but, no matter what, they were never going to fear us. Even though they knew we had good players and had enjoyed good results, they had been All-Ireland champions a few years before. And we were still *only* Antrim.

That played into our hands because it opened the door a little bit wider for us. It didn't matter if we had won against a good team the week before. It didn't matter if we had given them a scare the last time we played them, or even if we had beaten them… it's so hard for the bigger counties to shake the idea from their head that… *Sure, it's only Antrim.*

We could use that to sneak up on them.

And the semi-final against Offaly was ripe for a sneak attack.

OFFALY DIDN'T START like they were going to be caught at the finish.

Mark Corrigan got the first point after about 30 seconds. He had scored 3-7 against Kilkenny in the Leinster final and was a real danger man. After that first 30 seconds, he only scored two more frees and never got a look-in the rest of the match. James McNaughton completely shut him down.

Donal Armstrong equalised, but they went back ahead from the puckout and started to look like they were hitting their stride. They knocked over three more in-a-row and were hitting wides too. They ended up with 14 in the first-half but most of those were bad shots they were forced into because of the pressure our defence was putting them under.

I didn't really have anything to deal with and had caught a ball that came in after a couple of minutes and cleared it. It was good to get an early touch like that and, after Offaly had gone four points up, everyone started to settle into the match.

'Sambo' got our second point, and 'Beaver', 'Humpy' and Donal Armstrong scored as well, as we began to become the better team. Maybe it was nerves at the start of the game that caused our slow start but pretty soon everyone had contributed something – made a clearance or a block, taken a score or played a good pass – to get ourselves into the game.

We were two points down when 'Hippy' burst out from full-back and cleared the ball out towards Ciaran Barr under the Hogan Stand. Ciaran ran along the line and hand-passed up to Brian Donnelly, who swung the ball over his shoulder and towards the Offaly goal. It dropped onto the corner of the square on top of their corner-back Aidan Fogarty. Then, out of nowhere, 'Cloot' climbed above him and grabbed it out of the sky.

John Troy came out and dragged 'Cloot' to the ground.

PENALTY!

'Beaver' stepped up and gave the Offaly men on the line no chance. We were ahead for the first time and in the perfect position to push on.

Twenty seconds later, we were behind again.

Joachim Kelly won the ball from Troy's puckout and lobbed it in towards me. A couple of balls that came in before that, I had taken them and hand-passed them out for Dessie Donnelly to run onto and clear from corner-back.

This ball wasn't coming in very fast or from a big height, so I got ready to bat it out for Dessie. Instead, I batted it against the upright and it fell straight to Vincent Teehan on the edge of the square… and he buried it.

It was a kick in the teeth.

We'd played our way into the game, gotten ourselves ahead and, just like that, I made a mistake that let them back into it. Dessie came in to me.

'Look, forget it. Next ball counts!'

The next ball was a sideline that slid across the goal and I had to put it out for a '65', but thankfully they missed it and I dealt with the next one safely and felt I was back on track.

'Beaver' scored another point before half-time, but was it probably Offaly's best spell and they moved into a four-point lead at the whistle. We were disappointed to be that far behind after how we'd played, but Michael O'Grady made sure we wouldn't feel sorry for ourselves – or start to doubt ourselves.

'I'm glad I'm sitting in this dressing-room and not the Offaly dressing-room!

'In the second-half, this game is going to work out for us. The game-plan is working and we're going to turn this game!'

He was so sure, and that lifted us as soon as we went into the changing room. We believed him and when we went out for the second-half we had no doubt we'd be coming off the pitch with an All-Ireland final awaiting us.

But there was still a lot of work to be done.

A COUPLE OF minutes into the second-half Ciaran Barr whipped over a point off the ground, and then a minute later 'Sambo' swung another one over. With Offaly already four up we wanted to avoid the sort of slow start that we had had in the first-half.

We had it back down to two and were up and running.

'Cloot' scored a free after Offaly got their first point in the second-half. Then James McNaughton collected a ball out on his wing in his own half. He sent it in on top of Brian Donnelly and 'Cloot' in the full-forward line, as they jostled with their men. Just before the ball dropped, 'Cloot' spun around and backed away.

It was like he knew exactly what was going to happen. Being 'Cloot'... he probably did. The ball broke down... right to him and he scooped it up... before lashing it past Jim Troy.

The moment I looked down from the Canal End and saw that ball hit the net, I knew we were going to win. That put us a point ahead and it just felt that the day was shifting in our direction.

Everything seemed to be coming into place.

The gate had opened just enough and that day was the day we were going to pile through it. After years of waiting, this was the time.

'Beaver' scored and that point kind of summed up just how much it was our day. He ran through from the wing and hand-passed the ball inside. His pass was off target, but the ball bounced straight back to him and he put it over the bar.

Everything seemed to run our way like that in the second-half. A lot of breaking balls were bouncing for us but I'm a firm believer that you make your own luck in that situation, because if you're not in that position then the ball won't come to you. Even so, we seemed to have a fair rub of the green in the second-half.

Maybe we were cashing in on all those other years when all the luck we had was bad luck.

I had very little to do in the second-half except puck the ball out – and with our backs not letting Offaly get many shots in, I didn't have much of that to do either. Dessie made two or three really good clearances – it was no surprise when he ended up getting his All Star that season – and the rest of the defence coped well with everything.

The only thing that gave me something to think about was when Joe Dooley got a ball at a tight angle and drove it at the goal. I put my stick up, but thankfully it went over the bar.

That brought them to within a goal, but I landed the puckout right on top of Brian Donnelly on the 20-metre line and he knocked over a point. Our forwards were causing them problems every time the ball went down there... and 'Beaver' got another point to put us five up.

Offaly pulled a couple back, but I wasn't worried.

We were only a goal ahead, but all of our defenders looked comfortable on their men. It was a different story at the other end. Then Offaly manager Pat Joe Whelahan brought on his son, who was still only a minor at the time, for his championship debut – a young fella called Brian who would end up on the Team of the Millennium.

But nothing was going to stop us.

We got a sideline on the Hogan Stand side and Dessie Donnelly played it in to 'Humpy' in midfield. 'Humpy' doubled it across to the other wing and Ger Coughlan got out to it first, but Ciaran Barr barged him off it.

He tried to get a shot away, but Coughlan had got back to half-block him. The ball spun out to Brian Donnelly, right on the sideline... between the 20- and the 13-metre lines.

Brian fired over a dangerous looking ball, but it was 'Cloot' who turned it into something special. He was behind Aidan Fogarty on the edge of the square, but caught the ball, landed on his knees... somehow bounced forward, and smashed it past Troy.

When that hit the net, we were six up and everyone in Croke Park knew we wouldn't be caught. But confidence isn't the same as complacency, and a six-point hurling lead in injury time is hardly safe, never mind with eight minutes left.

I may have been convinced we were going to win, but it took one more goal until I could finally relax.

AFTER OFFALY PULLED a point back, I dropped the puckout right down on top of Ciaran Barr and Ger Coughlan, and Barr stuck his hand up and grabbed it over Coughlan's head. Just like he said he would.

Ciaran put the ball in and their full-back came out to collect it... but missed it. 'Beaver' was steaming through from centre-forward.

He picked up the rolling ball, rode a tackle and unleased a bullet past Troy. I had the perfect view of 'Beaver' going straight down the middle and hammering in the goal.

When it hit the net, it *hit* me... *We're in the All-Ireland final!*

The rest of the match was a blur and when the referee blew the final whistle it didn't feel real. After so many years of trying, we had finally got there. For all the belief we had in the panel, it was still a massive thing to take in that moment.

I collected my sticks and headed for the middle of the pitch, shaking hands with Offaly players. I remember Pat Joe Whelahan coming over... and I had a word with Ger Coughlan, whose brother had died in a drowning accident in America the previous week.

When the team gathered around midfield we shook hands, and hugged and slapped each other on the back. But I honestly think most of us were in a bit of a daze. Because Galway and Tipp were on after us, we couldn't hang around for too long, so we headed off towards the tunnel... between the Canal End and the Hogan Stand.

I was almost into the tunnel and off the pitch, when I realised the Offaly players were standing either side, clapping us off in a guard of honour. Whenever that match is spoken of or written about, that gesture from Offaly is always mentioned – and rightly so.

They had All-Irelands and Leinster titles and had already shown what sort of hurlers they were. That day they showed what sort of men they were!

After we had beaten St Rynagh's in the All-Ireland final with Loughgiel, any time were down to play Offaly the St Rynagh's lads always made a point of coming over and talking to us Loughgiel boys.

I always thought it took balls to do that, because if they had beaten us I might have said 'hello' but I don't know if I'd have gone over for a chat. I'd maybe have preferred to crawl into a hole.

Aidan Fogarty always made sure he would come over and talk, and here he was again, after a tough afternoon on 'Cloot' and just after losing an All-Ireland semi-final... standing with his teammates and clapping us off the pitch.

Pure class.

YEARS LATER, I was watching TG4's *Laochra Gael* programme about Pete Finnerty. He said the day after the semi-finals he was sitting in the pub, feeling sorry for himself, as the punters picked over Galway's loss to Tipperary.

He heard someone say about Tipp... 'They'll get a handy one in the final anyway!' He wasn't sure what he was hearing.

'Don't tell me Antrim beat Offaly?'

'They did!'

He said that made him feel even worse, which is fair enough... most teams would rather play us than Offaly. Galway were going for a three in-a-row and I'm sure Pete Finnerty was totally focused on his game, and after it was massively disappointed, but the fact it took him a day to find out we had beaten Offaly shows how everyone just assumed Antrim wouldn't be reaching the All-Ireland final.

Everyone except us.

« CHAPTER 11 »

WHEN WE SAT down for dinner that Sunday night, we were still pinching ourselves. We usually stopped at the Carrickdale Hotel on the border, on our way back up from Dublin, and for years we'd sat down for that meal with the same feeling.

This time it was different, and I don't think we really knew how to deal with it. It probably wasn't until the following week, when I was at home and sitting thinking about what was ahead of us, that I realised what we'd just done... and that we were in the final... AT LAST!.

People were coming into the shop and congratulating me, and I'd call in to The Pound where there was more of the same. For a few days at least, we could wallow in the Offaly win. Liam McGarry played the match on a loop on a big screen in The Pound.

When I watched the match again it gave me a chance to talk to 'Cloot' about what had gone on at the opposite end of the pitch to me.

After seeing how he had won the ball for the penalty, I asked him about it.

For 'Cloot' it was simple.

You're always told as a forward that you have to be out in front of your man, and the boys out the pitch are told that the best ball for corner-forwards is a low ball, drilled in. 'Don't be hitting in a big high ball,' you're told. 'That's a defender's ball.'

But sometimes, you can't help it and the ball will drop down on top of you. So 'Cloot' explained that when the ball came in high, his attitude was... *If that's a defender's ball, then I'll just become a defender.* So, he would step back behind his marker and attack the ball like he was a defender, not a forward.

Once he had it, he was a forward again.

'Cloot' was a genius, he could do anything. But he didn't just rely on his natural ability. He thought about the game and had a deep knowledge of it, and how to use that to give himself the best chance of succeeding. Some of the things he said made me sit up and think, because they had never crossed my mind.

Having a knowledge of the game is all well and good, but there are some things you can't teach.

When I asked him about his second goal, he explained it like it was obvious. 'There was no way I was going to go through my man, so the only way I could get a shot off was to throw it up and jump round him in mid-air.'

To 'Cloot' he was just doing the only thing he thought he could do. To him it was obvious. To everyone watching, he was doing something that looked impossible.

That was 'Cloot'

A VIDEO RECORDING was the first chance my dad had to watch the Offaly match. He couldn't go because he had been involved in the renovation of the chapel and work in the graveyard in Cloughmills, and that day a Mass was held to bless and rededicate the building. He loved his hurling, but his faith was very important to him and though he was disappointed not to be in Croke Park, he needed to be at the Mass.

The chapel was packed and Fr Stephen McBrearty, who was a family friend and had been Loughgiel's chaplain for our All-Ireland season, announced from the pulpit that we had beaten Offaly... to roars from the congregation.

By that time, Fr McBrearty had left the parish, but came back for the special Mass. He was awarded an MBE in 2019 for his work as a prison chaplain, and has been close to our family for 40 years. His uncle Tommy Kelly was one of the selectors with the Antrim minors and when we needed a pitch for a warm-up, before we beat Kilkenny in 1980, Fr McBrearty, who was in St Kieran's College at the time, got us one at the famous hurling school.

I think it was the following year that Fr McBrearty came up to Cloughmills (and Dunloy) as his first parish, and Tommy told him to come into our house and introduce himself. He's been a good friend of the family ever since.

He taught me how to drive and, like me, was a big music fan, so we went to concerts together. I loved Queen and Fr McBrearty got us tickets to go down and see them in Dublin at the RDS. But the same day, I was meant to go to a ceremony to pick up an O'Neill's Sports Star Award.

Still, that was during the day and the concert wasn't until a bit later that night, so I thought I'd be able to pick up the award, then we could head across Dublin to the concert.

But the awards kept going and *going*, and the start of the concert kept getting closer and *closer*. Eventually I had to say, 'You may go on ahead without me, or both of us will miss it'.

The thing was still going on when he got back... that's how late it was. I got my award but I didn't get to see Queen, and it turned out that I never would.

It nearly broke my heart.

JIM NELSON WAS one of the men – like my dad, Gilly McIlhatton, and Con Grego – who were always around Antrim hurling, whether it was as a manager, selector or administrator. Jim took over as minor manager after I had gone into the seniors, and was in charge of the under-21s as well as being chairman of the hurling board and an occasional senior selector.

Jim had already done a lot for the seniors with his role as chairman of the county hurling board. If it hadn't been for that hurling board, we would have got *nothing*. We felt as if we were viewed as a liability because any money that was being put into Antrim was put into the football team.

We were the poor relations until we made the breakthrough. Then, all of a sudden, we got what we wanted, and the footballers were the poor relations... which wasn't fair either. But before that, the county board did nothing for us. We weren't allowed to train at Casement Park, and we couldn't get a jersey at the end of the year, while the footballers were walking away with a bag full of kit.

When we were struggling in Division Two and looking like Division Three sometimes, if it hadn't been for the hurling board there probably wouldn't have been an Antrim hurling team.

Jim was hurling board chairman when Sean McGuinness quit and he stepped into the senior job like he had been waiting for it all his life, which in some ways he was.

While other managers made their contributions to building Antrim into something at the top level, Jim seemed like the perfect man at the perfect time to bring it all together. He brought a professional approach to the management of the team, which was something we had never really experienced before.

Jim's philosophy was that a *happy* team was a *good* team, and he tried to keep us happy – within reason. He looked after us because he knew that the fewer things we had to worry about, the more we could concentrate on our hurling and the better we'd perform.

If anything went wrong, Jim would try to right it. He told us if we had any problems, even a problem at home or something that had nothing to do with hurling, we should come to him.

Jim would try to take the stress out of things for us. If boys were coming straight from work to training, he'd make sure they could get there, get them fed and he'd get them home.

If I made a mistake, Jim never tore strips off me on the pitch, and the press didn't get the chance to do that either because Jim would take the blame for *everything*. If we didn't perform, Jim took the blame – but, once he got us indoors, he let us know why we didn't perform.

He was tough to play for but, because he treated us like adults and tried to keep us happy, we had huge respect for him. We were all friends with Jim, but there was a cut-off point where he had to become the boss… and we knew where that point was.

He could give you a telling off in a nice way. He didn't rant and rave, but he got his point across. He'd sit you down and tell you that you shouldn't have done this or should have done that. And because Jim was the way he was, you listened… and he wouldn't have to tell you twice.

One of the biggest things Jim did was to really bring us together as team. We had always gotten on pretty well during my time with the county, but when Jim started there were still the old divisions between clubs, and also between players from north Antrim and from Belfast. Jim was adamant that we weren't a collection of boys from different clubs, we were one team… WE WERE ANTRIM.

He made sure everyone mixed with everyone else, and took us on training and bonding trips that really achieved what he wanted them to.

We'd head down to Murlough House in Dundrum and, just as important as the training, was the time spent watching old matches… or a film or playing cards. We'd sit all night laughing our heads off and enjoying each other's company.

It's a big reason why we're still good friends more than 30 years later.

Whenever my dad was manager, he used to bring Jim in to talk to the panel. Jim and my dad were great friends and my dad always reckoned that no matter how good you were as a manager or a coach, a new face and a new voice every now and again helped, especially when the voice was as knowledgeable as Jim's.

Jim also saw the value in bringing in different opinions and fresh perspectives. Michael O'Grady was a great example. Jim brought him in to fine-tune and lift our level before the semi-final against Offaly.

O'Grady didn't teach us anything we didn't know already, but the way he coached seemed to improve all of us. At the start of training, he would tell us what the drill was and what it was for… while we thought to ourselves that we already know how to do this! Once the drill started, we realised we maybe didn't know how to do it after all… at least not the way we should be doing it.

Hurling is a game of basic skills and the better you want to be, the quicker you have to do them. The skills are the same at junior level as they are in an All-Ireland final – it's the speed that changes. O'Grady's drills got us doing these things we'd always done, but faster and *faster,* which meant better and *better,* and because he was able to keep things fresh, we didn't get bored and drop our standards.

And no-one was a better motivator. When O'Grady told you something you absolutely believed it.

'Believe you me, come tomorrow night every one of you boys will be household names!'

PETER FINN WAS the man who had the job of making sure we were in shape. He was a coach for the Northern Ireland Commonwealth Games athletes and was part of the backroom team when St Mary's, Belfast had won the Sigerson Cup.

Peter's athletics perspective was completely different to anything any of us had experienced. Until then, we had been running around a pitch. Peter taught how to train properly – how to *run* around a pitch.

Our training sessions in the run-up to the All-Ireland final were at club grounds, often before a club match, and people were coming out to watch us. All of a sudden, we were getting crowds to watch us training and, if you put on a match between Loughgiel and Cushendall or something as well, we'd have 3,000 or 4,000 people watching us run around the pitch.

On nights like that, we'd be self-conscious about it, because he had us running in a particular way that didn't look like the way you'd see anyone running on a hurling pitch. Peter wanted our stride and our arms to be right, so we were using our muscles properly and could build fitness more efficiently.

Though all we could think about was that we were running round this pitch looking like fools as 4,000 people laughed at us. But Peter knew what he was doing and he had us fit to last 100 minutes… never mind 70. With time running out, we'd have plenty more to give, and that was thanks to Peter.

As well as Dan Turley on the medical side, Jim brought in Dr Alasdair McDonnell, who went on to become the leader of the SDLP and an MP – the first time we ever had a dedicated doctor working with us. Before that, we would just drink bottles of water to keep hydrated, but he had tubs of peaches and glucose and salt tablets to keep us right, and try to prevent injuries like cramps and other muscle problems, and he looked at our nutrition as well. Jim had all the bases covered.

A picture that would become famous was taken after we beat Offaly, with Jim being chaired off Croke Park by Dr Alasdair and Oliver Kelly, the county chairman. Some county teams succeed despite their county chairman, but Oliver definitely deserves credit for contributing to our success.

He came in at the top of the county board in 1985, succeeding Hugh McPoland, and my mum told me that after the meeting was done, when Hugh passed my dad outside the room, he told him, 'Well, Neilly, you got what you wanted'.

It was true. My dad was a big supporter of Oliver, because he knew that he would give the hurlers a fair shake. That started when Sean McGuinness was in charge and, along with Jim Nelson and the hurling board, he went to Oliver to get more for the hurlers.

When Jim took over as manager, he and Oliver worked together the way you want a county manager and chairman to work together.

The day we played Offaly in the league down in Birr, I was to travel down with Oliver that morning. I wasn't feeling great as my dad dropped me off at Oliver's house in Belfast.

As well as being a prominent GAA official, Oliver was a prominent solicitor and worked in a lot of Troubles-related cases, so he was a target for loyalist paramilitaries. He had been told he was under threat, so rather than staying at his own house he would stay somewhere different each night.

We were outside Oliver's house, waiting for him to show up and my dad told me, 'You'll get the hairiest trip of your life down to Offaly'.

All of a sudden, a car came flying round the corner.

Oliver had arrived. My dad headed home, probably laughing to himself about what I was about to go through, and Oliver took me into the house. Oliver went upstairs to have a shave before we headed down the road.

I was sitting at the kitchen table with the blinds open, and I noticed that the blind in the window of the house opposite was going back and forward. I moved my chair away from the window... and kept waiting for Oliver.

My dad wasn't wrong.

We headed off down the road... and Oliver was flying.

I could travel anywhere, and had gone the length and breadth of Ireland plenty of times in the car, but this was too much. Halfway down we had to stop, and I got out and threw up by the roadside.

I'm still not sure how I made it to Birr in one piece.

MICHAEL O'GRADY WAS right.

We were household names all of a sudden and because that's all people knew – our names, or in some cases just nicknames – the press, especially from down south, had a huge appetite to find out more.

It seemed like every day there was phone call after phone call to the house, or journalists and photographers showing up at the shop. I seemed to be the focus of a lot of it, which I suppose isn't surprising.

I was distinctive, to say the least, and the fact I was a musician meant they had that hook as well. I found myself on the other end of a lot of interviews. Some of them were great – you got to talk to nice people who were interested in hurling and just wanted to hear what you had to say. But because a lot of them wouldn't have known one Antrim player for the next one, and hadn't bothered to write a single word about us or ask us a single question before now, we got more than our fair share of what I would say was *unfair* press.

I felt some of them were trying to make fun of us, like we were a novelty act up here coming down to play the 'real' teams. They were up to 'fill a page' and they didn't really care how they did it.

When some of the southern reporters who didn't really deal with us that often were talking to us, it was all light-hearted stuff. We trained as hard as any other county, we were playing in the same competition as these other counties, but they didn't treat us the same way they treated other teams.

They'd never ask Ken Hogan the same sort of questions they were asking me... or Nicky English the same sort of questions they were asking 'Cloot'.

The exposure we got was crazy from the day we beat Offaly... we didn't get a minute's peace. It felt like the phone in the house just never stopped ringing and when the press turned up to the shop with a photographer, as well as an interview they'd be looking for photographs of me serving customers.

The TV cameras were there looking for the same.

I was used to it a wee bit, maybe taking a phone call from a reporter before a game, but nothing like *this*... and I don't think there was one fella on the team who managed to avoid it.

The intensity of it was the main problem.

It was constant for the four weeks between the semi-final and the final. The day after the Offaly match, things just went through the roof and we weren't used to that. In retrospect it probably did make us take our eye off the ball, but we didn't realise it at the time because we were in the middle of it. I think Jim realised it after the final because he changed the whole way we dealt with the press and how they talked to us.

He'd arrange press nights in the future and, once that was over, that was it, we could get on with concentrating on the match. If that had happened in 1989, we probably would have put up a better show. It wasn't the reason we lost, but when you're preparing for an All-Ireland final, everything has to be right.

TICKETS WERE ANOTHER headache we could have done without.

We got 10 each... but if we had 50, I doubt it would have been enough to satisfy everyone. We were dealing with a lot of big families and, as well as everything else, the players had to field all these requests from people looking to get to the match. Instead of focusing on our game or Tipperary, we might be working out tactics on how to satisfy everyone who had asked... 'Any chance of a ticket?'

I think that's something else Jim would have changed, if we had got back to another final. The players would have been taken out of that scenario and been allowed to concentrate on getting ready for the game. But like the situation with the press, everyone's a genius in hindsight.

Not everything in the build-up was stressful.

We were able to enjoy a lot of it too, and Jim tried to strike the balance between protecting us from all the hype and letting us soak up the atmosphere that came with being in the All-Ireland final. We had been training in Loughgiel one night and headed over to The Pound afterwards, when we heard that the RTE cameras were up to film some stuff that would be shown on *Up for the Match* the Saturday night before the final.

We had to be hidden in the lounge, out of the way while they were filming in the front bar... in case it looked like the players were out for a session the night before the All-Ireland final!

It was great that my dad could enjoy it all too. Like most things, he wouldn't actually tell you he was enjoying it, but I could see he was in his element. He lived for hurling and had been involved with Antrim teams all his life, and never got to see one reach an All-Ireland final. Now, with me being on the team, he was still involved in a way.

Reporters and photographers were coming to his house to talk about the All-Ireland final. There were a few pictures of him in the papers and you can see it on his face... I could tell without him *telling* me.

We tried to have a bit of craic among ourselves in the squad as well. Before the final, we went down to Croke Park for one of the football semi-finals, a kind of dry-run, but more just another chance to get used to the place and the atmosphere. We were sitting together and had an experience we never had before – people were coming up to us looking our autographs throughout the match.

'Sambo' was at the far end of the line and someone, I think it was James McNaughton, said, 'Right, boys, everyone in the row... get your programme and pass it down the line to 'Sambo'... and get him to sign them.'

So, all these programmes found their way down to 'Sambo' for him to sign his autograph. Wondering why he was so popular all of a sudden… 'Sambo' looked up to see us killing ourselves laughing.

AND THEN WE had the song.

I couldn't tell how many teams have released songs before the All-Ireland final, but I know I played guitar and sang lead vocals on one of them.

John Watt, who's known as The Singing Farmer, phoned me and told me he had written a song for the team, and he said it would be great if we could do it. I listened to the song and spoke with Jim about it… and he said, 'Go ahead and record it'. It was to help as a fundraiser for the training fund as well, and we planned it so that it wouldn't take away any time from our preparations.

I went over to the studio in Dunloy during the day and did my bits, and then when we were training in Dunloy one night a lot of the boys came in afterwards and sang the chorus.

We are the Saffron county and we're gonna make our mark;
We'll take the Liam MacCarthy Cup to Antrim from Croke Park;
There will be celebrations in the city and the glen;
And we'll shake the hands of everyone, we are Jim Nelson's Men.

From the outside, it might have looked like we were getting carried away with everything and taking our eye off the ball, but it was one of the best things we did in the run-up to the final and did us no harm at all. It was good craic and it was an escape from some of the pressure and the nerves that were building.

We didn't uncover any hidden talents. Ger Rogan's not a bad singer and on trips down the country on the bus, 'Rogie' would keep us entertained with some Dean Martin numbers, but none of *Jim Nelson's Men* were heading for a career-change any time soon.

AS USUAL, WE stayed in the Grand Hotel in Malahide the night before the final.

We tried to keep our routine as close as we could to the way it always was. That meant heading down to the hotel and, coming straight off the bus, having a puck-about in the grounds. We were in the biggest game of our lives, but we played hurling because we loved it. It was the same when we were younger and the likes of Brian Donnelly would meet at our house and we'd hit the ball around to each other while we were waiting on the bus to take us to a match somewhere down the country or at Casement Park.

In Malahide, we used to be hunted through the garden because we'd be hitting the ball through flowerbeds and some of the boys would be taking the heads off the flowers. We had to go out around the side to the car park, until we were chased out of there too… we were endangering the cars. We were just mad to play hurling.

One thing that wasn't part of our routine was that our captain Ciaran Barr was getting married the day before the final. It was in Meath, where he was marrying Lynn Carolan, whose dad Pat was on the first-ever Meath team to win the football All-Ireland in 1949. It was just one of those things. The wedding had maybe been planned for two years.

I'm sure Ciaran had thought he'd get married the day before the All-Ireland final, go watch the match… then head off on honeymoon. But we put a spanner in the works and Ciaran had a big hand in that himself.

It probably wasn't until after we had finished playing that we realised just how good a captain Ciaran was. He had great faith in his own ability for a start, which you need if you're going to be a leader. You can't expect boys to do things you can't do yourself. There was no hiding behind the door when things had to be done. If something needed to be done, Ciaran was the first boy who would put the hand up.

If I had to puck a ball out into a fire… Ciaran would have stuck his hand in to get it.

We would have our meeting on a Saturday night before a game and, we would be ready to go to bed… and then Ciaran would step up to talk. We'd be thinking… *Ciaran, shut up, we've to get to bed here. There'll be time to talk in the morning.* But he always said something that stuck with you, something would help in the match the next day.

Ciaran had the privilege of spending his wedding night with all of us, and the squad went to Shelbourne Park greyhound stadium that Saturday night. With it being the night before the All-Ireland, Shelbourne Park was busy.

We had gone from *unknown* to *well-known* in the space of the month and a lot of people were coming up to us and asking for autographs. I was embarrassed by that sort of thing back them and was quite shy. Then two fellas came over and asked me to sign their programme.

'No bother, who's it for?'

'Morgan Kelly!'

I was in awe of Morgan Kelly, the Laois goalkeeper. All those top-class goalkeepers from different county sides when I was just starting… like Kelly and Kilkenny's Noel Skehan… Galway's Michael Conneely and Offaly's Damian Martin… men I wanted to emulate.

'No bother. I'll sign yours if you sign mine!'

He couldn't believe it.

'Are you serious?'

I couldn't have been more serious.

We had all been given £60 each to tide us over for the weekend, and I think I lost everything on the first race. The winner of the English Derby had come over and was an odds-on favourite, but got stuffed. I only found out later on that Micheal O Muircheartaigh, the RTE radio commentator and a big greyhound man, was there giving all the other boys tips. That would have been good to know.

I hoped backing that loser would use up all my bad luck for the weekend.

« CHAPTER 12 »

FOR MORE THAN 30 years, I couldn't think about the 1989 All-Ireland final without thinking about one split second… and nothing else.

I could remember little details from the day – the biggest day of my hurling life – and how I was feeling at different times as we played Tipperary in Croke Park. But, no matter how hard I tried, I couldn't stop the whole experience being reduced to that single moment.

We were losing by three points, but hadn't long gotten our first score.

It was almost exactly halfway through the first-half and we were doing okay. Tipp hadn't blown us away like most people thought they would.

We had missed a few decent chances too, and had shot five wides. You could tell we were a bit nervous, but you could tell Tipp were as well. They were playing *Antrim*. Surely the match should be *over* by now?

Then Declan Ryan picked up the ball about 30 yards out… and hit a shot.

He didn't get hold of it properly, so instead of sailing over my head for a point it came dropping towards my goal.

I put up my stick.

I ALWAYS TRIED to treat every game I played in as just another game.

Some players would maybe get keyed up for certain games, or be on edge for every match they played, but I always found myself on a pretty even-keel, whether

I was playing a league match for Loughgiel... or an All-Ireland semi-final for Antrim.

I've gone into big games trying to make myself nervous because I think you need to have some nerves... to be on that edge to perform. I've gone out to some games thinking... *I need something here to get the adrenaline going, to make myself nervous.*

But there were a couple of times that I didn't need to do that. I was nervous enough to play the 'wrong way' after winning the toss in my first Antrim final and, on Sunday, September 3, 1989, I didn't need to do it either.

That morning, I was as nervous as a kitten.

'Sambo' was feeling the same and the pair of us went for a walk up around Malahide, just a dander along the water to get our heads cleared. We might have met one or two supporters but there weren't that many, and any we did meet just wished us all the best in passing and that was it.

There was no standing talking to them, and anyway, we wouldn't have known what to say.

The nerves disappeared as the bus, complete with a garda escort, took us from Malahide to Croke Park. The month since the semi-final had brought a few new experiences, but speeding through Dublin... up one-way streets, through red lights... with four police motorbikes in front of us and four behind was like being on a different planet.

We were buzzing as we zoomed through the streets.

As we got closer to Croke Park and the crowds started to get bigger, things got a little quieter. Some reality was setting in.

We got into the ground and into the changing room, and ready to head out onto the pitch. It all passed in a blur. I can't remember a word Jim Nelson or Ciaran Barr... or anyone else who might have been talking said.

I can remember the noise.

Back then, the tunnel was in the corner between the Hogan Stand and the Canal End, and when it was our time to leave the changing room, Ciaran led us running out onto the pitch... and I was there behind him.

The first thing I saw was Hill 16, covered in saffron flags... but the sight wasn't what hit me first... it was the sound. It was like firecrackers going off... it almost knocked us off our feet as we came out of the tunnel. And it didn't stop!

IN THE FIRST-HALF, I was keeping goal in front of the Hill, and all those Antrim supporters were chanting and shouting non-stop for the 35 minutes. I couldn't hear a word from my defenders, and I may as well have been howling at the moon when I was shouting at them.

I could barely hear *myself*. It was deafening, and nothing like any of the semi-finals, not even the Offaly match when the place was full.

But it wasn't just the sound!

Running out onto the pitch, the whole atmosphere hit me in the chest.

There was something different in the air. When we came out, we were supposed to meet in a huddle, and Jim or Ciaran was to speak to us. So, we got together and then somebody said, 'Where's Sambo?'

He was standing way up in his position at corner-forward, all by himself. In different ways, I think the occasion was getting to all of us.

I PUT UP my stick.

Declan Ryan's shot had risen just enough for the ball to get into the sun, and that's where I lost it. It spun off the edge of the stick and settled behind me in the net.

As I turned and picked it up, the umpire waved his green flag and, for me anyway, the All-Ireland final was over.

If you asked me the next day what had happened in the rest of the match, I don't think I could have told you. If you'd tried to tell me the next day what happened in the rest of the match, I wouldn't have listened.

That mistake… my mistake …was the *whole* story.

It wasn't until I watched the match on TV more than 30 years later that I allowed the memories of the rest of the All-Ireland final back in.

A MINUTE AFTER their goal, 'Cloot' caught a long ball into the full-forward line and hand-passed in to Brian Donnelly, who was on his own on the 20-metre line. Brian drove his shot just over the bar.

Nine times out of 10, Brian would have buried that in the back of the net but I think he decided to make sure of his point, to keep the scoreboard ticking to keep us in it. We'd hit all those wides at that stage and had only scored a point.

We *needed* another one.

But Tipp were starting to play like they'd had a weight lifted off their shoulders – and it was the goal I had let in that lifted it. They were getting on top and taking their scores, and we were finding it hard to get any of our own.

They threatened for a couple more goals, but I managed to stop one from Nicky English, and collected and cleared another when Cormac Bonner came through and hit me on the side of the head… although the TV commentators said I had taken a dive.

Tipp were 11 points up at half-time, and there was no way back.

They didn't slow down in the second-half and got another couple of goals. Tipp were dominant and able to cruise to the end, but our forwards gave their defence some tough moments in that half.

'Beaver', Brian Donnelly and Donal Armstrong all scored goals in front of the Hill and gave our big support something to shout about.

'Beaver' got the first one and set up Brian for his. I played with 'Beaver' from under-14s right until the end of my career. Whenever we were playing with the club, Paddy McIlhatton would have stepped out to the side at centre-back, the midfielders split… and 'Beaver' put his hand across his chest as a signal for me to drill the ball at him chest high.

And if I hit a ball to 'Beaver' it would almost always end up in his hand.

If a defender was giving him a hard time, he'd give me another signal… a finger up in the air. That was my cue to drop the ball down on top of him. He didn't try to catch that one. He'd pull and if he hit the ball, well enough, but if he didn't the centre-back would know he was there.

If you wanted to hurl with 'Beaver', he'd hurl… if you wanted to mix it, he'd mix it and could run through anything.

In the first few minutes of the All-Ireland semi-final against Offaly, he took a blow to the head that would have sidelined most players. But the blood was wiped from his face, he got patched up and he went out and scored 2-4 to help get us to the All-Ireland final.

WE WERE 15 points down and I could feel the Tipperary supporters who had managed to make it over and through the Canal End fence behind me, starting to gather along the end-line. Out in midfield a ball broke to a Tipp player ,who hit a long ball up over our full-back line and right into the path of Nicky English.

The ball bounced up for him and he caught it perfectly. As it hit the net, it felt like the whole Canal End had poured past me.

For God's sake, ref, I thought. *Just blow it up.*

After they cleared the pitch, he did... and that was the cue for the supporters to come back on and celebrate their All-Ireland.

Our All-Ireland was gone.

The supporters on the Hill stayed to cheer us, and we made our way down to thank them. I was in tears, and I wasn't the only one.

Paddy Quinn, who was the Rossa goalkeeper at the time, put his arm around me and talked to me all the way back up to the tunnel. If he hadn't been there, I don't think I would have made it off the pitch.

We were the big story going into the final, but afterwards it was all about Nicky English. He ended up scoring 2-12 – a record for an All-Ireland final that still stands. There were some Tipperary players who just didn't show us any respect; they never had, whether it was when we had played them in the league or the year before in the championship, or in the build-up to that final. And things would get even worse afterwards.

But Nicky English wasn't one of them.

After I made the save from him in the first-half he gave me a tap with the stick, to acknowledge me. He did it a couple of times during the match and you could tell he wasn't doing it to try to wind me up or patronise me.

I'd played against him enough to know he wasn't that kind of fella.

He was hurling's biggest star at the time and I know I used to look at the players from counties like Tipp, Cork or Kilkenny and think they had it easy, especially compared to us up in Ulster. We were just *nobodies* playing away at our hobby and they were well looked after, getting cushy jobs from the county and whatever else.

It was only when I read Nicky's autobiography years later that I realised that just because you're a big star from Tipperary doesn't mean everything has come easy. He played for a small hurling club that was mainly interested in football, and whenever Tipp were going through bad patches the press down there would be merciless with him.

You don't have to be a hurler from Antrim to have obstacles to overcome.

My sister, who lives in Ballina, was at a dinner dance he was a guest at and when he found out who she was, he introduced himself and asked if he could have his photo taken with her. I've met him a few times since the final and he's a genuinely lovely fella.

I wasn't so fond of him on the day of the final, though. They were winning everything out the field and once the ball went in to him, everything he did came off. First Gary O'Kane, and then James McNaughton, couldn't do anything to stop him.

And if those two couldn't, I doubt any defender could have.

AFTER THE MATCH, there was some talk that it was a mistake to start Gary, who was 19, on English but it never entered our heads that Gary wasn't the man for the job – and he was up for the challenge.

In the end, it didn't work out but we were one hundred percent behind him. We were one hundred percent behind every man on the team to do their job, no matter who they were marking or who was marking them.

We believed in each other, and if it didn't work out one day, we still believed in each other the next day.

Gary went on to be one of Antrim's best-ever players. The following year, I went to see Dunloy playing, just to watch Gary O'Kane.

We were in line to play them in the championship and Gary was the centre-back, so I wanted to see how he operated and how I'd have to plan my puckouts against them.

I knew he was good at reading puckouts, but I had it my head that he could be a wee bit suspect if the ball was dropping directly down on top of his head. I had the idea that he sometimes got under it a bit too early. So I went to see if I was right.

I couldn't have told you one thing that happened in the match if it didn't involve Gary O'Kane. I couldn't have told you who won. But I came away shaking my head.

Before the other goalkeeper hit the puckout, Gary was on his way to where it would land, and he caught just about every one of them. I went to the match thinking I could maybe find another couple of weaknesses to go with the one I thought was there already.

I left it thinking he didn't have any.

BACK THEN, THE day after the All-Ireland final, both teams met for a banquet at Kilmainham Gaol. We had had our own post-match reception with our own people and our own families already in Malahide and the last thing we wanted was to be hanging round Dublin.

We wanted to get back up the road…back home.

That's how we felt before we got there. We had lost, we hadn't done ourselves justice. It always got my goat that people were saying in the run-up to final that we had nothing to lose. We had the *final* to lose.

Sure, Antrim aren't expected to win, so why would they be too upset if they lose? Brian Donnelly's reaction when Mick Dunne had asked him if we really thought we could win the final was the answer to that. I would have been the same – we all would have been the same. None of went out thinking about anything but playing our best hurling… and winning.

Losing hurt, and we were going to Kilmainham for a banquet with a team that had just beaten us by 18 points in the All-Ireland final. And it was nothing against Tipperary – we just didn't want to be there.

It wasn't all bad.

During the match, I had asked one of the umpires to keep me a ball so I could take it home and give it to my dad, but he told me he couldn't do it. Then at Kilmainham, he came and handed me the ball. It was nice of him to do that.

I was asked to come up and sing *The Green Glens of Antrim* but I didn't want to do it. So, our kitman Henry McCabe got up and my jaw dropped. I had never heard Henry sing a note before and then out comes this big, deep baritone voice.

But we were never as glad to get on a bus as we were that afternoon, because it's a miracle the gaol didn't see a riot break out. They may have been great players but some of the Tipp boys were nothing but ignoramuses.

And just calling them ignorant is being generous to them.

Making jokes about us, trying to belittle us… not showing us any respect. You could have cut the atmosphere with a knife. I think at one stage PJ O'Mullan had one of them by the throat. After constant abuse, 'Hippy' offered some of them outside for a conversation with all the Donnellys.

I know who my money would have been on.

And it didn't stop there! The following month, the Railway Cup was being played over a weekend down in Wexford. I had quit playing for Ulster because I was busier with the band and just didn't have the time. Eddie Donnelly was the manager and Noel Keith from Down was the goalkeeper, and Eddie asked me if I could come down to Wexford, basically to drive the Loughgiel boys and also sit on the bench as the substitute goalkeeper.

Eddie needed a car to take boys down from Loughgiel and also someone as back-up in case anything happened to Noel... and I killed two birds with one stone for him. I told Eddie it was no bother. I wouldn't expect to be doing anything but driving the boys down and up for the weekend.

Ulster played Munster in the semi-final on the Saturday, and Noel got a crack on the head and I had to come on. We were playing well and beating them by six or seven points. James McNaughton was marking Nicky English, and this time Nicky never hit a ball. James was brilliant that day.

But then he went down with a knee injury. He had torn his cruciate ligament and the surgery ended up keeping him out for nearly a year. That day, Munster came back and got a draw... and then ran away with it in extra-time. It was the closest Ulster had got to a Railway Cup hurling final in nearly 50 years.

A Connacht team that was made up of Galway players beat Munster in the final and back at the hotel a few of us got talking; some of the Ulster players and a lot of the Galway boys, and we were just having a good time. John Commins, who I grew friendly with, was there and so was Eanna Ryan and a few others.

I was sitting talking with John and chatting about how we were coached and what way we trained. Goalkeepers swapping notes. There was a piano there too and everyone had a bit of a sing-song. And one of the same crowd from Tipperary, who had been ill-bred at Kilmainham, came up to me and just started talking to me in Irish... knowing I didn't speak Irish.

'If you're going to speak to me, speak so that I understand you.'

But he kept going.

'If you don't stop, I'll drive you out that window.'

I was raging, because he was only doing it to try and show me up. John said to me, 'Look Niall, forget about him. I was standing going to the toilet and he came in and tried to make a fool out of me too'.

We were sitting there, having a good time with the Galway lads, the craic was mighty, but someone else decides they'd get their entertainment trying to belittle someone else.

I would still have a dislike for Tipperary because of that, which is a shame because it was a few players out of a team that contained some real gentlemen. Back at Kilmainham the likes of Nicky English, Michael Cleary and others couldn't have been nicer. They were lovely fellas who could commiserate with us, without being patronising.

Genuine men, who treated us with respect – even though they'd just hammered us in an All-Ireland final.

BETWEEN 1986 AND '91, Antrim played in six All-Ireland semi-finals and were competitive in every one of them. We only managed to win one and when we got our 'final' chance it passed us by.

I honestly think getting to another final would have made all the difference to that team – maybe enough for us to actually win the All-Ireland.

If we had beaten Cork in 1986, or held on against Kilkenny the following year, then the experience of one of those finals, however they might have turned out, would have been massive for us in the years after. Reaching the final against Tipp in 1989 wouldn't have been the shock to the system it turned out to be.

They had reached the final the previous year – the first time any of their players had been there – so nothing was new to them. If we had that under our belt in 1989, we might have won... or we might not have, but we definitely would have stood a better chance. For about six years that team was good enough – our hurlers were good enough – but we just couldn't put it all together. And for Antrim to win an All-Ireland, everything has to fall into place at the right time.

After 1989, Jim brought in a press night to take the pressure off dealing with the media – and everything that was new and different when we played Tipp wouldn't have been a surprise if we'd got back to the final after that. It's why 1991, when Kilkenny beat us, stands out as a big missed opportunity.

If we had managed to beat them, like we should have, we'd have been going into the final against Tipp on a level playing field, and we would have been able to just concentrate on the hurling and playing the match. And maybe Tipp would have fallen into the old trap of... *It's only Antrim...* especially after hammering us in 1989.

We could have used that complacency to our advantage in 1989, but I had let that advantage slip away from us. Tipp were under a lot of pressure. They were such massive favourites that the longer we could stay in the game, the more the doubts in their heads might have grown. But the goal was a pressure release for them.

Once they heard we had beaten Offaly, as far as they were concerned their semi-final against Galway was the real All-Ireland final. They had been told for a month that the match was a foregone conclusion. Sure, they were *only* playing Antrim. If we had beaten them, they would have been the laughing stock of Ireland.

We wouldn't have thought that because we knew we had a good side, but everyone else would have told them that.

The year before, we gave them the fill of it in the semi-final. If we were still hanging around into the second-half, with most of the crowd getting behind us and their supporters maybe getting nervous too, who knows what might have happened? Maybe all those things would have fallen into place for us.

But because of me we never got to find out.

SO, WE HEADED up the road after the bad experience at the gaol, and not really knowing what to expect when we got to back to Antrim. A whole homecoming tour had been planned for the next couple of days, starting at Casement Park that night. We didn't know if anyone would be hanging round to see us at 11.0 o'clock at night, the day after the All-Ireland final… when we had no cup to show them!

The bus pulled off the motorway and onto Kennedy Way, just before you head up the hill and turn down the Andersonstown Road for Casement Park. They put us on a float, like a horse and cart, to travel the last bit of the journey.

The road was packed with thousands of people.

We couldn't believe it. Everywhere we looked, people lined the road. We went into an absolutely jammed Casement Social Club for some music.

And it was only the beginning.

The next night was north Antrim's turn and we left Casement and headed up the coast, calling in at all the hurling clubs along the way. We made our way through the Glens, stopping in Glenarm, Waterfoot… and then Cushendall.

As the bus pulled up to stop in Cushendall, wee Leonard McKeegan was sitting there on the bridge, official Antrim blazer and all, with a big smile on his face. No one had noticed he wasn't on the bus, but somehow, he had beaten us back to Cushendall and was sitting there on the bridge as we arrived, and clapping us off the bus.

Next it was on to Cushendun, Leonard included, and Ballycastle where you couldn't move in the Diamond – it was unreal.

After that it was on to Armoy, then Dunloy... then Loughgiel.

Every stop was the same. Everywhere you looked there were Antrim supporters – some who'd been down in Dublin all weekend and some who'd stayed up and watched it on TV, but every single one of them was cheering and singing, waving flags and patting us on the back.

The next night was the south west of the county – mainly football country – but the crowds didn't get any smaller. When we got to Randalstown, we stopped at a country club and went in where Eugene O'Dornan and Johnny Sayers were playing.

That night they managed to get me up to sing *The Green Glens of Antrim*. But when I was up on stage someone came running in and said, 'Come on... the bus is going!'

When I got out, the bus was away. Thankfully, somebody was able to give me a lift to Antrim town a few miles away, where the bus was stopping at the chapel, so I was able to get back on it.

Unsurprisingly, nothing had run on time. What was meant to be a half-hour stop here or there turned into an hour or more, and by the time we got to Glenavy it must have been pushing three in the morning. According to the homecoming timetable they printed in the paper the week before, we were to be in Glenavy for 10 to 10.

Of all the places we stopped, Glenavy was probably as far away from hurling country as you could get. But at three in the morning there was a band there waiting for us, along with hundreds of people. It was a cold night on the shores of Lough Neagh and hundreds of people had waited for hours for a team that had been beaten by 18 points.

Someone handed 'Cloot' an accordion and he led the band down the main street in Glenavy as we followed behind.

Seeing all those crowds, you asked yourself if you deserved it? It makes you wonder what sort of reception we would have got if we had done the job right. We went out and got destroyed, and people waited up all night to pat us on the back.

To say, 'Well done'.

And to say, 'Thank you'. I'll carry that experience to the grave.

PART SIX

'Excuse me, that's my son out there'

I remain so grateful to all of the amazing people who helped me to have the career I had with Loughgiel and Antrim – and who helped me to take my place on the greatest stage in the GAA... Croke Park on All-Ireland final day.

The morning of the All-Ireland final in 1989, we presented ourselves with our management team and the county board outside the Grand Hotel in Malahide. A band of hurlers... and a band of brothers!

« CHAPTER 13 »

BY THE END of 1989, barely two months after playing on the biggest stage in hurling, I didn't know if I'd ever lift a stick again.

Physically and mentally, I thought I was finished. The All-Ireland final had hit me like a tonne of bricks. As far as I was concerned, letting Declan Ryan's goal go in was the beginning of the end for Antrim's chances. That moment had set demons loose in my head. Those demons were telling me I had lost my nerve, that I wasn't fit for those sorts of days anymore... that Croke Park was no place for the likes of me.

I was also sitting with the worst injury of my career.

My right leg, from the knee to the ankle was a mess. I had been playing with the county for 10 years and there was nothing to say to me that I would play one more. But I wanted to. I wanted to because I loved it.

I wanted to because... I didn't know what I'd do without it... and I wanted to just show that I could.

THE LOUGHGIEL TEAM that won the All-Ireland in 1983 was a young team.

I was 21 and although there were a few veterans, like PJ O'Mullan, Paddy McIlhatton, Mick O'Connell and Brendan McGarry, the vast majority of us were in our early twenties. Looking back, we should have won more than we did, but the fact we didn't just shows how difficult it is. People don't realise how much it takes out of a group of players to reach that sort of level year-in, year-out. It's part of the reason I think so highly of that great Ballycastle team of the late-70s and early-80s – they were able to hit that level every time they went out in the championship.

By 1989, we had gone seven years without a county title – a long time for a team coming off winning the All-Ireland. Six weeks after we had won that All-Ireland we were back defending our Antrim title but that match against St Teresa's, and the next one against St Gall's, were against two of the lesser lights and we won easily without playing particularly well.

We were expected to do the same against Sarsfield's in the semi-final, but were lucky to get out of Casement with a win. Even though they had a man sent off in the first-half, we were heading out until Brendan Laverty got a ball in the middle of the field, ran through and burst the net with a couple of minutes left. When the referee blew the whistle, about three-quarters of the Sarsfield's team stood back and just nailed the boy beside them.

The sticks kept flying well after the match was over.

Ballycastle were waiting for us in the final and they wanted to knock the All-Ireland champions off their perch. In the end they did, but we should have won that match comfortably. We missed a lot of scores we'd normally have taken and were a point down when 'Woody' came through with the chance to tap the ball over the bar and get us a replay. But he went for the win, and Paul Smith stopped his shot at goal. He also came out with the ball and took it in his hand three times before he cleared it. Paul still talks about it, still laughs about it. We all would have tried the same – we all got away with worse.

By the time of the final, we had been training solid for two seasons. I think we ran out of steam. Because the All-Ireland final was delayed, we never really got the chance to come down, get the feet back on the ground... and reset. Instead of getting ready to peak again, we had to try to stay at that peak constantly.

In the end we couldn't do it... I doubt anyone could have.

The closest we came to the county title after that was when Cushendall – helped by Sambo's pool playing at the Athletic Grounds – beat us in the 1985 final, but by the time '89 came around we knew we wouldn't be far away.

PJ O'Mullan was the manager, and we had six players on the county panel and they were good... strong players in every part of the pitch. As a goalkeeper, sometimes you're only as good as your full-back line, and that team had a good one – with Paddy McIntyre at full-back and Liam Quinn and Damian Carey in the corners.

Our whole defence was strong and they made sure I didn't have many saves to make that year. But as good as I felt we were, there were plenty of other contenders for the title. Rossa were the reigning champions and had reached the All-Ireland final earlier that year. They played Cushendall, who had won the title the year before, in the first round and we were drawn to play the winners in the quarter-finals. By the time that match came around we had seven players on the county panel.

Armoy were meant to play Sarsfield's in the opening round of the championship but pulled out the week before the game. They were struggling for numbers and had already been unable to field a couple of times in the league. That meant Sarsfield's got a bye into the next round, but it also meant a man who'd end up as an All Star in 1989 didn't have a club to play for.

'Cloot' came to play for Loughgiel!

That might not have gone down well with some people in other clubs but 'Cloot' and his brother had played underage hurling with Loughgiel, when Armoy didn't have the numbers for a team, so it was only natural he'd come and play for us – at least that's what us Loughgiel boys on the Antrim panel were telling him.

He also played for Ballycastle as a minor in 1980 – the year Antrim could have won an All-Ireland and Ballycastle didn't send any players to the county. So, we were bending his ear to come to us... and the Ballycastle boys were doing the same. We had an ace card in Liam McGarry, who was a selector on the Loughgiel team that won the All-Ireland in 1983 and was very close with 'Cloot'.

I think Liam's powers of persuasion must have played their part.

Liam was Mr Hurling in Loughgiel, he just loved the game. Running The Pound bar meant he was at the heart of the community – and that means *hurling*. We'd be sitting in The Pound after training or a match and Liam would come out and say, 'Have a look at this, boys!' And he'd set up the video with the TV, and put on an old match.

Then, when that was finished, he'd put on another one. I had just called in for a Coke or whatever and, the next thing I know, I'm sitting there with Liam, six or seven other players and maybe a few supporters, watching these old games and talking hurling until two or three in the morning.

Liam could have done that all day and all night. He had hurling on the brain and went to something like 50 All-Ireland finals in-a-row.

And he could play as well. I remember my dad saying Liam McGarry was one of the best right-backs in Ireland and that, added my dad, was… 'When hurlers were *hurlers*!' He played in 14 county finals and won six, including two when he was next to my dad in the full-back line.

Liam's view of the game was simple – but very effective. If you wanted to annoy Liam it was easy… hit a short puckout. Aidan McNaughton used to have a habit of slipping to the side to open up the middle of the field, which meant I could then find somebody in the half-forward line coming back looking for the ball, because Aidan had left a gap for me. When Liam saw that happening, he would start shouting at me.

'HIT THE BALL… AS FAR AS YOU CAN!'

His philosophy was to get the ball as close to the other goal as quickly as possible and if a goalkeeper can do that with one swing, why would you want to do anything else? I'd say to him, 'But if I can get a ball to a midfielder… or a half forward coming back into midfield, he can stick it over the bar'.

'Maybe!' he said. 'But you're putting him under pressure and it's too close to your own goal to be doing that in case he loses the ball. Then the other team can stick it over the bar.'

I wasn't going to change his mind.

He usually got his way anyway, and nine times out of 10 I'd try to hit the ball as far as I could every time, which was the way the game was played then anyway. But Liam wasn't just saying that to be traditional or because he was stuck in his ways. It was the Loughgiel style and it had served the club well down the years.

It obviously didn't do us any harm in 1983 when Liam was a selector. Liam was just one of so many experienced, knowledgeable people in our club who passed that on and helped us be successful in the future. People like Liam and Johnny Coyle gave us a great grounding in the game, how it should be played – as it was in those days – and those things never left me until the day I finished.

EVEN THOUGH THE arrival of 'Cloot' obviously made us a stronger team, we were still the underdogs when we went over to play Cushendall, who had knocked out champions Rossa.

The first-half was a tight one and we were one up at half-time.

Then 'Cloot' scored a goal early in the second-half and we pushed out to a nine- or 10-point lead. But there was still plenty of time left and, after Dominic McMullan went off injured, Cushendall started to come back… got two goals and, all of a sudden, there were only a couple of points in it again. Thankfully, we were able to settle down after that and hold on to win by one in the end.

Now we had a semi-final against Dunloy to look forward to, but Antrim's run meant we'd have to wait more than three months to play them.

Over in the other side of the draw, St John's were already sitting waiting in the final. They had surprised Ballycastle the same day we beat Cushendall back in June, and because they didn't have any players on the county panel – and neither did Sarsfield's – they could play their semi-final while our match against Dunloy was put on hold. They had nearly two months to wait and play the county final, while we had two games in eight days.

So, two weeks after losing to Tipperary, we lined out against Dunloy in Cushendall. They were the up-and-coming team in Antrim hurling at that time. They'd won nearly every underage title going for the past few years, were that season's under-21 champions and were looking to win the club's first ever senior championship.

The chat was that this young Dunloy side was going to run us ragged and pump holes in us. We would have liked our chances anywhere but it did help us that the match was in Cushendall. The pitch there was on the smaller side and my puckouts were nearly landing in the square. That took a lot of things that might have been in Dunloy's favour out of play, and they didn't have the room to exploit us.

They also had to do without their one county man, Gary O'Kane, while our other six – I played well enough – were on top form. We had a strong wind in the first-half and put the foot down from the start. Dunloy couldn't handle 'Cloot' and Sean Paul McKillop, and we were flying.

We were 12 points up at half-time, and ended up winning by nine.

The final was the following Sunday at Casement Park, and we were up for it. Even though we'd won an All-Ireland, we'd gone so long since winning in Antrim that we really appreciated what a county title meant. Yes, we can have a go at Ulster or the All-Ireland if it happens, but that county title is the first thing and was really *everything* for us at that stage. There was a still a buzz round the county after the All-Ireland final, which brought a wee bit of added incentive. If people thought about Antrim hurling, they'd think about 1989... and we wanted to be county champions that year.

The matches St John's had played to get to the final – against Ballycastle and Sarsfield's – were rough, tough clashes. Gerry McClory, my old minor manager, was the referee and said to me after the match that all the talk round Belfast was that St John's weren't going to take any prisoners. They would cut us to ribbons to win the championship. Gerry said it took him about two minutes to realise it wasn't just St John's who were thinking like that.

Every ball was fought for by every man. We knew St John's weren't going to take a backward step, so we didn't either. I don't think there was one half-hearted tackle from either side. Some of them were just good, hard challenges, but some of them were nasty. Five men were sent off – three for them and two for us – but there probably could have been twice as many.

Not all the nasty tackles were punished, and not all the red cards were for bad tackles, but thankfully we were able to keep our heads and won well in the end.

'Cloot' and Sean Paul McKillop were the stars again and scored a goal each. The St John's defenders tried everything they could – fair and foul – to stop them, but they couldn't manage it. We were those two goals ahead at half-time and pulled away in the second-half.

WE WERE THE Antrim champions for the first time since we were All-Ireland champions, and straightaway attention turned to repeating what we did in 1983. First up was the Ulster final down in Portaferry – a huge challenge.

The problem was, the week before the Ulster final, the National League was due to start again and Antrim were playing Kilkenny at Casement Park. With the county team reaching the All-Ireland final, there weren't too many times we all trained together with the club. The club was able to have us once the Tipp match was played, but when the National League started getting closer a row started brewing between the club and the county management.

The club's view was simple... *The county has had our players all year, trying to win the All-Ireland. Now it's our time to try to win the All-Ireland... and we need our players.*

Loughgiel wanted to pull the players out of the match, but Jim Nelson wouldn't hear tell of it. They managed to hammer out some sort of deal and, in the end, I think maybe three Loughgiel boys played against Kilkenny, with the rest on the bench.

I was one of the ones who played – and I was happy to. I'd been lucky with injuries through my career and, anyway, the chances of me getting hurt as a goalkeeper compared to an outfield player were minimal.

There was a big crowd there to see us – and Kilkenny too, who hadn't been up in Antrim for a match for the guts of a decade.

I played grand – I kept a clean-sheet – but Kilkenny scored 20 points and we were not able to live with them. Their sub goalkeeper from the year before was the man who did the damage on his first outfield appearance for the Kilkenny seniors – a boy called DJ Carey. But how I played, and even the result, didn't matter. Not as much as an innocuous ball dropping from the sky.

'Hippy' was playing full-back and was marking Christy Heffernan. A ball came in from out the field and I followed it all the way into my hand and then – CRACK!

'Hippy' and Heffernan were jockeying in front of me and, as 'Hippy' pushed Heffernan out of the way, he pushed him into me and his full weight, knee-first, came down onto my right ankle.

There and then, I knew that whatever had happened wasn't good. It turned out to be torn ligaments, a cracked shin and an Achilles tendon stretched to breaking point.

I went straight from Casement Park to the nearby Royal Victoria Hospital, where they wanted to put me in plaster, but with an Ulster final now less than a week away I wouldn't let them. So, they bandaged me up as tight as they could and sent me home.

Once I was there, I sat with my foot up on a chair, wrapped and iced for the next seven days. Before the match against Portaferry, Tommy Armstrong, who was training us, took me for a fitness test and told me I wasn't fit to play.

'I'm playing!' I said.

So, the management agreed that I would start the game and come off after 10 minutes once the full-back line was settled. 'That's fine!' I said, knowing full well I wasn't coming off that field until the final whistle.

The match was every bit as tough as you could expect it to be down in Portaferry. The big crowd got a beautiful, sunny afternoon and a thriller. Thankfully, it was the Loughgiel supporters who got the result they wanted.

It didn't look that way for most of the match, and Portaferry got a couple of goals in the first 20 minutes and were ahead by a goal at half-time. They were still leading about midway through the second-half, but we were playing better by that stage, especially at the back, and they never scored again. We only managed three more points ourselves but we kept things tight and, in the end, won by two.

As soon as the final whistle went, I went straight to the pavilion, sat down and cried. They weren't tears of joy... they were tears of pain.

I never saw 'Woody' being presented with the cup.

I'd play another four years with the club and county, win Save of the Year and be nominated for an All Star, but playing in that game was the biggest mistake I ever made. I was never the same after it. But at the time, you're not thinking about that. *There's an Ulster final on Sunday and I'm playing in it.* That you could hardly walk for the week before it never entered your head. But that's what you did – and it's only when you think about it that you realise how stupid you were.

The only serious injury I'd had was also my right ankle, five or six years before at club training when I stepped in a pothole and damaged a ligament. That kept me out for 13 weeks and my first game back was against Dunloy. My cousin Eugene Trainor, God rest him, was playing for Dunloy and hit me a crack on it.

I went down and my dad came onto the pitch to see what had happened. He thought I had gone over on it, but I said, 'No, Eugene hit me there by accident!' My dad wasn't having it. 'THAT WAS NO ACCIDENT...'

But this felt different. After I left Portaferry that day, I wasn't sure if I'd ever play again. I knew the ankle was bad when I was sat in the hospital the week before, and I knew I had made it worse.

But I didn't want things to end that way.

ANTRIM DIDN'T WIN a match for the rest of the league, and I didn't play in any of them. After the Kilkenny game, we lost by a point to both Wexford and Tipp, and then fell away to some heavy defeats.

I missed the matches before Christmas because of the injury, but I had recovered enough for Loughgiel's All-Ireland quarter-final against Desmonds from London at the end of January. The weather was awful leading up the match and it looked like it might not go ahead. In the end, it was played but our pitch was a mess and it was shifted up to Carey, about 20 minutes away.

We knew from playing London teams so often down the years that they were going to be no pushover and, on the morning of the match, John McKinley, 'Woody's father, died suddenly.

We struggled through the match, against the weather and the opposition. It was level at half-time, with only a few points scored each, and they had missed a penalty. We managed to get our act together after that and a couple of goals had us 10 points up late on. They pulled back a couple of goals of their own and, in the end, we won by five points, but knew we'd have to improve for the semi-final.

The weather hadn't improved by the time we played the Limerick champions Ballybrown a fortnight later. I don't think it stopped raining for those two weeks. Our pitch hadn't got any better since the Desmonds game – it was still a mire – but home advantage for an All-Ireland semi-final was obviously considered too valuable to give up. It wasn't a surprise that the match was a dour struggle. I don't think I can remember a game where I had less to do. I never touched the ball all day except for my puckouts. No shots to stop… no balls to catch.

The wind was howling, and they decided to play against it in the first-half. As they'd done all through the championship, our big names were delivering. 'Beaver', 'Cloot' and Sean Paul McKillop all knocked over points and we led at half-time, but only by four points… with that wind to face.

Neither team was making many chances and the difference ended up being long-range frees they scored, while we could only manage one point in the second-half. We had chances – their 'keeper stopped one from 'Beaver' late on, and we had a chance from a '65' right at the end, but it just wasn't going to be our day. Their last free, which turned out to be the winner, bounced over off the post.

That Loughgiel team could have won an All-Ireland. Hand on heart, I don't think that team was as good as the 1983 team, but I still think it was good enough to win it. We knew what was needed to win an All-Ireland and we had it that year.

That was one that got away.

THAT I WAS able to get back on the field at all was thanks to Dan Turley. I'd go up to Antrim training and get treatment there, and other nights I'd go up to

Dan's house. I worked hard because I was determined to get back and show I wasn't finished, but Dan really did work wonders. That was the physical side. Alec Emerson from Cushendall had come in as a coach that year and, when I was fit to, Alec worked with me a lot to help get my confidence back.

My goal, while I was out, was to get back to Croke Park and try to put things right from the All-Ireland final. In 1990, we'd be playing the Munster champions in the All-Ireland semi-final, so there was every chance it would be Tipp again. But first we had to get past Down in the Ulster final, and that was getting harder every year, especially now they had our old manager Sean McGuinness in charge.

I had managed to get myself back into the team for the final and had plenty to do in my first county match in nine months. We were missing a few boys through injury, like 'Hippy' and 'Sambo', and Down came at us all guns blazing… like we knew they would.

We had some hairy moments at the start of the match and eventually settled down, but we were still a point behind at half-time. They hit wide after wide at the start of the second-half but then, in the space of a couple of minutes, we turned things around. Sean Paul McKillop and Jim Close both scored goals… and Down were shell-shocked. We were well in control and when we got another goal, we thought that was that.

But Down kept on *coming*.

I had already made a couple of saves but, in the last few minutes, Down went into overdrive. We were six up… they needed goals, and I needed to stop three point-blank efforts. When the whistle went, we were probably more relieved than anything.

The following week we went down to Thurles to watch the Munster final, fully expecting – like the rest of the country – that Tipp would win and we'd be getting an All-Ireland final rematch. But Mark Foley scored 2-7 and Cork pulled off a massive shock. So, we wouldn't get the chance of revenge, but I'd still get a chance of redemption on the biggest stage.

As usual, Jim had everything covered in our preparation for the semi-final, but we went into the Cork match missing one of our best players because of a row over a bottle of water at training.

I didn't know it had happened until I came off the pitch, and was back in the changing room at Casement Park. 'Sambo' had missed the Ulster final through

injury and was watching us train from the side of the pitch. Anthony Mulvenna
– the hurling board secretary – had a bottle of water and 'Sambo' asked him for
a drink.

'Only players get water!'

'Sambo' didn't take too kindly to that and there was an altercation – and
later on, there was a suspension. Jim Nelson advised 'Sambo' to write a letter of
apology – whether he thought he had something to apologise for or not – but it
didn't make any difference. To the players, it just felt like the same old story with
Antrim. If the officials could find a way to make a mess of things, they would.

The week after we had reached the Leinster minor final in 1979 the entire
hurling executive – my dad included – had resigned over the fixing of club games
at the same time as county training and right before county matches. I don't
know for sure, but I wouldn't be surprised if Terence Barton and Ciaran Donnelly
getting sent off in a club game the week before our final had something to do
with it. It was far from the first or last time that it felt like the county board was
working against the county team.

We knew that if we did everything right, we would put ourselves in the
position of beating the top teams. After that it might take a bit of luck, or them
having an off day, or a bit of magic from someone like 'Cloot' to get us over the
line. But 'Sambo' being banned – especially over something like a drink of water
– felt like, as a county, we were shooting ourselves in the foot.

We had been around long enough to know there weren't many counties who
would go about things the way Antrim did. There were plenty of times we went
down to play Kilkenny or Cork on a Sunday, and you'd find out someone on the
other side had been sent off in a club match the evening before… and it never
made it into the referee's report

So, we went into the semi-final missing one of our top players when we had
no need to. It was already an up-hill battle and we didn't help ourselves by making
such hard work of it when we started against Cork.

They scored four out of their first five shots.

We scored none of ours! When John Fitzgibbon ran through and scored their
first goal after about 15 minutes, we were nine down. We weren't playing all that
badly… we just weren't taking our chances.

Everything they were hitting was going over. We settled into the game as it went on and 'Cloot' and Brian Donnelly got a couple of points each, but we should have been much closer than the seven we were down at half-time. We had hit 12 wides, mostly from men in positions where you'd have put your life on them to score. Ger Cunningham had made a good save from Noel Murray as well, so we were well in the game when we went out for the second-half. A couple of minutes later, Fitzgibbon ran through and gave me no chance for another goal.

The start of both halves cost us that semi-final.

Giving a team like Cork starts like that is always going to sink you. But that didn't mean we were going to give up. We hadn't given up against Tipp when they were running away from us the year before, and we weren't going to give up against Cork.

He might not have been the captain anymore, but Ciaran Barr showed his leadership qualities that day. 'Humpy' McKillen started getting on top at midfield as well and scored a great point, before Ciaran gave me the signal to send a puckout his way. He grabbed the ball, ran through and smashed it past Ger Cunningham.

We should have been *gone*, but instead Cork were rattled. 'Beaver' was tripped up when he was running through and 'Cloot' tapped over the free. Tony O'Sullivan got their first point in a while and then, in the space of 30 seconds, gave me the chance to show I could still be a goalkeeper on the big stage. First Kevin Hennessy broke down a long ball into the square and O'Sullivan pulled on it first time. I reacted well enough to get my stick up and stop it.

We cleared it down the other end, but Cork turned it straight back around and O'Sullivan had gotten completely free just outside the 13-metre line. He hammered it to my right, but I dived across and caught it on the first bounce… and got it away.

But even though we were finally playing our hurling, we never got closer than six. 'Beaver' had a half-chance at a goal blocked and Cork were able to take their points and add to their lead. In the end we lost by 10. If we'd even taken half our chances in the first-half it would have been a different story – but we knew every time we played against teams like Cork that we had no margin for error.

The way the game had gone meant we walked off Croke Park disappointed. Winning was the most important thing and we hadn't done it, but I knew I could at least feel I still belonged on the pitch on a day like that. At the end of the season, my first save from Tony O'Sullivan was nominated for Save of the Year…

the second one won it… and I was nominated for an All Star.

The last time I walked off Croke Park it had been in a daze.

I thought I had cost Antrim the chance of an All-Ireland. This time I walked off feeling far better about what I had contributed to my county's cause.

But I had no idea I'd never play at Croke Park again.

« CHAPTER 14 »

THE FIRST TIME I ever played at the 'Home of Hurling' – Semple Stadium in Thurles – was for the Antrim under-21s in the 1979 All-Ireland semi-final against Tipperary.

I was still only 17, the substitute goalkeeper and wasn't expecting to play. We weren't expected to come near Tipp either and that's the way it went. They scored four goals in the first-half and three more in the second. Our goalkeeper Francis Dick had to come off, so I was going to get my run-out.

As I ran on, I could hear them laughing.

And I knew what they were laughing at.

I WAS ALWAYS big.

From my first days playing hurling, until the day I retired, and in the days since, me and my weight have been in constant disagreement.

From my first hurling matches at underage level with Loughgiel, you'd get people sniggering or making comments over the wire. My mum would turn round and tell them, 'Excuse me, that's my son out there'.

I used it to inspire me as much as I could.

I knew they were thinking... *Look at the big fat boy in goals!*

So, my motivation was to prove them wrong, to go on and try to achieve something, to not let anything – including them and their insults – hold me back.

I was always a positive person in anything I did. I tried not to let set-backs get me down.

I wanted to turn them into a positive – a chance to learn something or a way to be motivated.

In later years, I saw goalkeepers like myself and I hoped I was a motivation for them. They've seen me do what I did and achieve what I achieved – captaining the All-Ireland club champions or reaching the All-Ireland final with Antrim – and hopefully they thought, *I can do that.*

It could be someone playing for a club team or a smaller county team – or any team. I always hoped that maybe I could inspire somebody like that just by going out and giving everything and trying to play as well as I could.

After we had finished playing, a fella from Ballycastle I hurled with for the county told me he had always admired me for the simple reason that I never let my size stop me achieving what I wanted to. It was very nice of him to say that. I didn't think we had that much in common; we never spoke all that much when we did play together and I wasn't in his company a lot, but I appreciated that he said that.

A big part in my career was to try and push myself on, and prove to people that I was able to do the sort of things I ended up doing.

There's no point in pretending my weight didn't affect my play, because it did.

My first year with the county, I'd lost a lot of weight and was playing well and my best years for Antrim were probably from 1982 to '87. I made no mistakes at all then and was so sure under a dropping ball. But then as I started to put weight on and get heavier, wee stupid mistakes crept in.

Jim Nelson had dropped me for the Tipp match in the league in 1989 because the weight had crept back up a bit. Jim had a habit of doing that during the league, if he thought weight was an issue.

He'd bring in whoever was sub goalkeeper at the time to give me a kick up the backside but, to be honest, it got to the stage that I knew when it came to the championship, as long as I was playing well enough, I'd be back in again. The effect of the kick up the backside wore off and I didn't lose the weight I should have.

Jim was trying to get the best out of me and I was maybe getting a bit complacent.

When Jim was back involved with Loughgiel in 2011 and '12, I had been going to Slimming World and had managed to lose five stone. I was talking to him one day and he said to me, 'You're looking in great shape… you're doing well, keep it up'.

And then he laughed and said, 'Where was Slimming World when I needed it?!'

I was never small, but the extra weight did make a big difference and, later in my career, it was getting to the stage it was affecting me, something that Jim could obviously see. I wasn't getting off the ground to catch balls that I used to, and I was making the odd wee mistake, which for a goalkeeper can quickly become a *big* mistake.

I used to be fit to come off my line among players, even 10, 12 yards off my line; I could have come out among five or six men and caught the ball in the middle of them. If a ball was coming in and heading over the crossbar, I could have risen and caught it.

It got to the stage that I couldn't do that anymore.

For Declan Ryan's goal in the All-Ireland final, maybe I did lose the ball in the sun, but it was probably in my head at that stage that it was the safer option to go at it with my stick. Two or three years earlier, I wouldn't have thought twice about getting up and catching that ball. The weight was starting to take its toll and make me think differently about how I was 'keeping.

It's part of the reason I thought my career was over in 1990.

Three bad leg injuries rolled into one, combined with the fact that I didn't know if I'd ever get my confidence back after the final. To come back and play the way I did against Cork, win Save of the Year and get an All Star nomination helped me prove something to myself, because there were times I thought I'd never lift a hurl again.

I DIDN'T WIN the All Star in 1990, but that wasn't my biggest All Star disappointment. 1990 was the second time I'd been nominated for an All Star.

The first was in 1983 after Loughgiel had won the All-Ireland and I'd made all those saves against Galway in Mullingar. I remember Justin McCarthy said I was certainty for it and was the best 'keeper in Ireland – but Noel Skehan had just retired after winning his ninth All-Ireland. When it came to handing out the All Stars, they gave Noel a record seventh award to go with his record ninth All-Ireland.

I could hardly argue with that. I was 21 years old, and Noel Skehan was one of my heroes.

1990 was different. By that stage I had been playing county hurling for 10 years. I worked hard and had some good years – as well as some bad ones – but I knew that, on my day, I was a good goalkeeper and in my two championship matches in 1990 I had done everything that was asked of me. In the Ulster final, Down really put it up to us and I made four or five point-blank saves in the last 10 minutes. Then against Cork in the All-Ireland semi-final, I made two saves reckoned good enough to be nominated for Save of the Year – and one of them won it.

But when it came to decide, Cork 'keeper Ger Cunningham beat me by one vote. Adrian Logan from Ulster Television came out and told me he had fought tooth and nail, but it was the 'Munster vote' that decided it. My saves against Cork obviously weren't enough – and Adrian was the only one who could talk about my saves against Down because the highlights never made it to the All Star committee. *And how else are a crowd of reporters from Cork or Tipp going to see the Ulster hurling final?*

John Commins was the other goalkeeping nominee, and I spent the rest of the night sitting with John, Adrian and a few others. With Cork playing the All Stars in Toronto, there would be a place as an All Star replacement up for grabs, because Ger Cunningham would be playing with Cork. I would have seen an All Star replacement as a big honour, because there weren't too many Antrim men on that list either.

'If I'm picked as the replacement for the tour,' John said to me. 'I'll say I'm injured and not available… because you deserve to go.'

'Thanks John, but no, I don't want it that way. If I don't get it… I don't get it!'

The weekend the travelling party was being announced my aunt Eileen, who lived in Canada, phoned my mum.

'I hear Niall's coming out to Canada. They read out the All Stars who were coming over and Niall's name was on the list.'

Happy days, I thought, *I'm getting a trip here as an All Star replacement.*

Then I got a phone call from Jim Nelson, who was managing the team picked by the All Star committee and he told me, 'I'm sorry, Niall, you didn't get it'.

'OK, Jim, that's fair enough. John Commins?'

'No… Jim Troy!'

I couldn't believe it. The Offaly goalkeeper was a good goalkeeper but he hadn't even been nominated for an All Star. *Why had they looked past the men who were nominated and picked someone else?* I thought I didn't fit the image the GAA wanted to show off over in Toronto. *They're not going to take me out because I was a big fat so and so.*

I'd just be a figure of fun and it hurt to think that was the case.

There was no All Star tour for the 1983 team, because the following year was the GAA's centenary, so the chance of a replacement was off the table back then. In 1990, I felt I had been denied the chance for reasons that were nothing to do with hurling.

It was a kick in the teeth.

WE WERE IN Division Two of the league, but it was the toughest Division Two we'd been in for years. Galway had gone down with us the year before, so we were stuck with the team that had just reached the All-Ireland final; Offaly, who were the Leinster champions, and a Down team who had shown in the Ulster final that they were banging at our door.

We ended up losing to all of them and never got close to challenging for promotion. I played in the matches before Christmas, but in the new year my ankle was starting to give me bother again and I wasn't fit for the last few games.

It was the second year in-a-row that I had missed more league matches than I played. I had put such an effort into getting back the previous year that I wasn't sure I could do it again, but this time the injury wasn't so bad and I made it back into the team for the Ulster final against Down.

Down had been slowly but surely creeping up on us.

They always had good hurlers – we knew that from playing against Ballygalget, Ballycran and Portaferry in the Antrim league – but they were starting to really put things together with the county. They had been promoted to Division One in the league and very nearly beat us in the Ulster final the previous year.

They also had Sean McGuinness in charge, and Sean was the perfect man to get a bit more out of Down. From a personal point of view, I had to deal with more than usual because Sean had brought in Tommy Armstrong, who had come in to coach Loughgiel a few years before – the first time I had ever had one-to-one goalkeeper coaching.

Tommy was a great coach and his drills had me in the best shape of my life. But because of that, Tommy probably knew my game better than anybody. He knew my weaknesses and after he went to Down, I noticed that their forwards would hit balls at me a bit differently.

I knew the Down forwards as well as anyone from the Antrim league and I could tell that they had changed. At the time, it didn't sit well with me that somebody I had worked with at club level was going to be giving away my secrets, but I suppose that's what happens, and Tommy was an excellent coach who was going to use all his knowledge to help the team he was with.

A few years later, when I was part of a management team going for the Loughgiel job, I asked Tommy if he'd come on board, but by then he had retired.

We knew Down were a serious threat in the Ulster final and there was no way we were going to be complacent. We knew what was coming and, if they beat us, it wouldn't have been because we were taking it easy. All you needed to do was mention Down and we were always up for it.

We started well – John Carson scored a goal in the first minute – but they got a goal of their own and we were only two ahead at half-time. 'Beaver' scored another goal for us in the second-half but we couldn't shake them off, and were lucky that they were hitting plenty of wides – and that they had two goals disallowed.

But it looked like our luck was running out when they were level with a minute left. That was when our experience saw us through. 'Humpy' scored a point and 'Beaver' scored a goal, and we got out of jail. It was an even bigger relief than the year before.

After the match, Sean came into the dressing-room and one of the boys said something like, 'Sure you're an Antrim man anyway Sean!'

Sean jumped down his throat.

'I'm a Down man today!'

The rivalry was only getting stronger.

I COULDN'T SAY the same for my ankle. It was still giving me bother and when it came to the All-Ireland quarter-final against Westmeath, Jim started Pat Gallagher. After we had struggled against Down, Westmeath fancied their chances against us but we hammered them out the gate. Unfortunately for me, Pat still got plenty of chances to show what he could do and he never put a foot wrong. When it came to the All-Ireland semi-final against Kilkenny, Pat deservedly kept his place.

I couldn't remember the last time I had watched a match from the bench in Croke Park. It wasn't easy – and it was made a lot harder by the fact we should have won. It wasn't like the Cork semi-final the year before, when we lost by 10 and had only ourselves to blame because we didn't take our chances. Against Kilkenny we were the *better* team.

They scored a goal after less than 30 seconds, when Eamon Morrissey ran straight through and kicked it past Pat, but after that we took over. Dessie Donnelly had struggled against Down and was dropped for the Westmeath match, but Jim knew what Dessie could offer on a day like that and, two years after he had turned him into an All Star corner-back, he moved him to his old spot at corner-forward. Fifteen minutes into the match, Dessie scored the sort of goal only Dessie at his best could score.

He got the ball near the end-line and, with barely anything to aim at, smashed a bullet past Michael Walsh into the net. That put us ahead by three – and we stayed ahead until Morrissey scored another goal to equalise with less than 10 minutes left.

We probably should have been out of sight at half-time. We were four ahead, but nearly had a couple more goals. 'Sambo' had a fantastic game – he was well worth his All Star at the end of the season – and we were dominating after half-time, even though they had the breeze. But we weren't making it count on the scoreboard and they chipped away at the lead until Morrissey's goal had them level... and then they went ahead.

'Sambo' equalised with a minute left, but Morrissey and DJ Carey got two injury time points and we were beaten.

Antrim have never been anywhere as close to an All-Ireland final since.

IT HAD BEEN hard to sit on the bench and watch the match.

I had hardly played the year before, but that's when I was injured. To be physically able to play but not be picked was difficult. I knew I would have to fight to get my place back but I also knew I didn't have a lot of *time to fight* to get that place. I was busy with the music and my injuries weren't getting any better, but I couldn't just walk away. I didn't want anyone to say I had retired because I didn't want to be a sub.

It took me nearly a year to get back into the team and, when I did, it didn't go well. We hadn't played Down in the league that year because they were in Division One and we were in Division Two, so when it came to the Ulster final, they probably wondered why they were underdogs as usual.

They definitely didn't play like it, and in the end beat us by 11 points when it could have been far more. It was a tough one to take, and it was made tougher by the fact some of Down players rubbed our noses in it by gloating after the match. I suppose they had played second fiddle for so many years and we were the Ulster giants there to be killed, but there was no need for that.

I had played on enough Loughgiel teams who lost to Down clubs to know they had hurlers every bit as good as Antrim had. Some of my best friends hurled for Down and even though it was a great rivalry whenever we went out on the pitch, I always had nothing but respect for Down hurling.

I WAS GOING to retire after the Ulster final, but Jim asked me to give it another six months so he could work another goalkeeper into the panel, and I agreed. I don't know if Jim was going to give me a start in the league out of sympathy, but the way it turned out Pat Gallagher was sent off against Offaly, so I got the No 1 jersey for our match against Down.

After the 1989 All-Ireland final, I wasn't sure if I'd get back to the top level again. After I was injured against Kilkenny, I didn't know if I'd play again.

I had managed both against Cork the following the year, but after that match I think I knew that, however slowly, time was running out. I ended up playing three more matches for Antrim, all of them against Down.

After the third of those, I knew I was gone.

I had a stinker. We lost, both their goals were probably my fault, and I walked off the Casement Park pitch to tell Jim I was finished. I couldn't face the time when Jim would come over and put his arm around me, and tell me that I wasn't up to it, that it was over.

I wanted to make that decision for myself, get out on my own terms.

'That's it!' I told Jim.

'I'm not going to put you through that again... or put myself through that again!'

I went into the Casement social club and it was obvious I was in bits. Boys were coming up and patting me on the back, and saying, 'Just forget about, it was one of those games... next time will be better!'

But I was so upset, because I knew there wasn't going to be a next time. Jim knew it too. When I told him I was done, he didn't try to talk me out of it.

THAT WAS IN November 1992.

I always thought that if I quit county hurling, I'd maybe play one more year with the club and that would be it. I enjoyed hurling as a youngster because there was no pressure. I came into an Antrim team with a few fellas the same age, looking at older players I wanted to emulate. But when I was in their shoes and got to their age, it just wasn't the same.

I didn't enjoy it the same way.

I don't know if I felt more pressure or just that I didn't fit in with the younger lads. The Loughgiel team was changing too. In 1990 we lost our county title when Rossa beat us in the semi-final. That was bad enough, but then they went on to lose to Dunloy in the final – the first time Dunloy had ever won the county title.

For years, that was the reply any Loughgiel person had to whatever Dunloy folk threw at them, 'Come back when you've won the championship'.

Now, they finally had won the championship, and we could have stopped them.

Cushendall and Ballycastle beat us in the next two semi-finals. My generation was starting to retire, and I felt out of place. The injuries didn't help.

Carrying a niggle on a trip down to Cork or Waterford... and back on the bus – with sitting on the bench in between – meant I couldn't walk the next day.

I turned 31 in January 1993.

The following month, daddy died.

WE THOUGHT WE'D lost him 10 years before.

He had bowel cancer and was given six weeks to live. I went in to visit him in hospital, but I only went in the once. He was always a big man, but he had lost seven stone and looked like a skeleton lying in the bed. It was too much for me.

I honestly thought he would be coming out of hospital in a coffin.

He was let out of hospital to see us play Ballycastle in the county final. He sat up on the steps in Dunloy in a wheelchair with a blanket around him. We didn't do anything to make him feel better by losing our Antrim and All-Ireland titles, but he defied the doctors' prognosis and managed to recover.

A few years later, he started having problems with his heart. His seat for the All-Ireland final was right at the top of the Hogan Stand, and he really struggled up those steps.

I had to take him into hospital two or three times. One night I took him in, every window in the car was open, but he couldn't get a breath. He was clinically dead when we got to the hospital, and they had to revive him.

A week before he died, Paddy McShane, who hurled for Ballycastle, and Eamon McGarry, who hurled for Loughgiel, landed up at the house with a full bottle of whiskey. I don't think there was any left by the end of the night. They sat and talked about the old days, about the games they played against each other and with each other... and going to dances and meeting up at each other's houses for a game of cards. Whenever they left, my dad was sitting smiling with big rosy cheeks on him, and it wasn't just the whiskey.

He couldn't have been happier if you had handed him a thousand pounds.

I had just started playing with 'Pandy' Walshe and our first gig together was on New Year's Night 1992 in the Village Inn in Dunloy. My aunt Eileen was over from Canada and she came out along with mammy and daddy to hear us playing.

My dad said to my mum that he'd never seen me look as happy on stage. I had no idea I'd end up playing with 'Pandy' for so long, but my dad obviously saw something that very first night.

Six weeks later, we had a wedding in Cookstown and dad was back in hospital for a few days with his heart. I called into to see him on the way down to the wedding and he was in great form. They were letting him out later that night, and he looked well. He had actually helped one of the nurses put a man into his bed and he was waiting for a doctor to make one last check on him before he could go home.

I was on stage when a phone call came through to the hotel.

'Come home. Daddy had a heart attack... he died!'

I couldn't believe it. I got into the car and pointed it for home. Somewhere along the road, I was pulled over by the police.

'Do you know what speed you were doing?'

'I don't!'

I could barely answer him, I was in bits. He could see there was something wrong and asked me what had happened. I told him my father had just died, and I was trying to get home.

He let me go, but told me to take my time or I could be next.

Dad was only 63 when he died on the 22nd of February 1993. His funeral was two days later. He was buried in the graveyard right behind the house in Cloughmills, with my stick next to him in the coffin.

It was Ash Wednesday.

MY DAD WAS a part of Antrim hurling for decades.

It's obvious from talking to people who played with him and under him, and served on committees with him, that he was respected everywhere in the county. The Antrim County Board named the Under-21 Championship trophy after him and any time I chat with anyone who knew him they only have good things to say.

He could get the best out of you, whoever you were. He knew who to put the arm around and who to tear strips off, but he would never give off in front of other people. If he thought you needed talking to, he would have taken you to the side.

Seamus Richmond told me that at half-time in one match my dad took him into the shower and tore strips off him.

'You've been atrocious – are you going to let that boy walk over you all day?'

Seamus was taken aback, but he went out and turned the tables on his man. 'Your dad knew that would get my gander up and I'd go back out to prove him wrong. After the match, when we had won and I came back to the changing room… your dad was standing there smiling.'

'Well, Seamus?'

'Well, Neil… you were right!'

JP McFadden wasn't long on the team, and before he went out for one match my dad took him to the side.

'See the man you're marking? Get up in close to him and take a good sniff. See what he had for his breakfast?

'If you can smell a fry off him… you take him for a few runs round the field.'

JP said he laughed at that but, when he got out, sure enough, he got a whiff of bacon and eggs off his man. It wasn't the last time JP checked to see what his man had been eating for breakfast. Sometimes, he'd smell a fry… the odd time it would be a bit of drink from the night before.

But it was always the cue to go running, and to give Antrim or Loughgiel the best chance of winning.

He was a great man for tactics, but it wasn't all about putting men in the right place or playing a certain way. I can remember sitting in the changing room before a county final with Loughgiel. The biggest day of the year and the nerves were starting to build.

The next thing, a wee bottle of whiskey came out of my dad's pocket.

'Have a jig of that to settle yourself.'

We were playing a match somewhere way down the country with Antrim, maybe Carlow or Waterford. We all headed down in a fleet of cars and I was sitting in the back seat of one of them, right next to a window that wouldn't close. By the time we arrived at the hotel, I was shivering, so I was sent straight to bed after downing six paracetamol and tin of Coke.

When I woke up the next morning, the bed was drenched.

I had sweated most of whatever I had out of me, but I still wasn't right. So, we went out to play the match and my dad gave me a wee jig of whiskey. Between the tablets and the drink, I didn't know where I was.

But we won the match and I managed to keep a clean-sheet. I thought the defence must have been very good that day because I didn't remember making too many saves. We headed back home up the road and I fell into bed… exhausted.

When I woke up the next day, I found about 15 ball marks all over me… my chest, my arms… my legs. I must have been just stepping in front of balls and not realising what was happening. Thank God, I didn't have to worry about a drugs test.

My dad was happy with the clean-sheet.

Not that he told me. That just wasn't his way.

He was hard on me, to try to get the best out of me, and though sometimes I would have wondered what I had to do to please him, I knew how he was and accepted that even if he was happy I wouldn't hear about it.

He let it slip once… but only because he didn't know I could hear him.

It was hard for him to hide how pleased he was after Loughgiel won the All-Ireland. It was maybe quiet satisfaction, but if you knew him, you could tell. About a week after the final, I was coming into the house and I could hear him on the phone.

'Oh, yes… I'm very proud of him!'

I had no idea who he was talking to – or who he was talking about, but it turned out the phone call was to tell me I had won the B&I GAA Personality of the Month award – a prestigious thing at the time. I was the first-ever hurler from Ulster to win it, and only the third hurling goalkeeper after the great Seamus Durack from Clare and Noel Skehan from Kilkenny. It was a great honour, but hearing my dad say he was proud of me was special.

Deep down I knew he was, but hearing it was nice.

I probably didn't appreciate at the time how lucky I was to spend so much time with my dad. From growing up and travelling round the country with him at his work, to the hurling with Loughgiel and with Antrim, I was with him a lot more than a lot of young fellas. The fact he was involved, especially with the county, meant *two long days* away down the country somewhere weren't two long days away from him that, when he was gone, I might look back and regret.

Of course, when he died it hit me hard.

It's something that never leaves you, it only changes – but I'm grateful we had those times together, and I'm grateful to hurling for that.

I honestly thought that my dad dying would kill my mum too. They were very close. They used to kneel at the side of the bed every night to say the Rosary together. They were truly soulmates.

But she got through it, and in October 2021 she turned 89 and is fresh as a daisy. A few years before she fell and broke her femur, but was back on her feet in nine months; no walking stick, *nothing...* up galloping around again.

I'm the one who has to keep up with her. We'd be over in Dunloy visiting the graves and I tell her, 'Mum, you walk wild fast!'

'I have to keep fit!' she'd reply.

DAD WAS GONE, and I wasn't involved with the county any more.

I had a fair idea 1993 would be my last year, but as the season went on, I just couldn't find the enthusiasm for the game I had had since I was no age.

We played Cushendall in the county semi-final and things couldn't have gone much worse. They scored a goal after a couple of minutes and got another two before half-time. We were *nowhere* all over the pitch and, in the end, we lost by more than 20 points.

Hand on heart, I wasn't to blame for any of the goals that went past me.

I've made enough mistakes to have plenty of practice holding my hands up to them, but that day it wouldn't have matter who was in the nets. For one of them, 'Sambo' came through from centre-back and ran all the way up the field with nobody near him. I stopped his shot and someone came in and stuck the rebound in the net.

I could see our manager telling the substitute goalkeeper to warm-up. Thank God, I made it to half-time. I don't think I could have faced having to walk from the goals to the sideline. But being substituted, even in the privacy of the changing room, was a kick in the teeth.

I knew I was finished. The last match I'd play for Loughgiel that year would be the last match I'd ever play.

I missed a few league games with gigs but was able to play against Ballycran in Loughgiel. It wasn't the last game of the season, but I knew it was for me.

I must have played well because some people came up and patted me on the back after it, and I remember a woman came up to me and shook my hand and said something nice about me and Noel Keith – Ballycran's brilliant goalkeeper and a great friend.

I thanked her mentioning me and Noel in the same breath.

I put my sticks in the car and drove out the gates. After longer than I could remember, I wasn't a hurler any more.

« CHAPTER 15 »

BEFORE WE WERE married, Naomi and I were away in Spain on holiday.

There was an Irish music night on nearby so we went along and at some point, she got up from the table to use the bathroom. When she got back, she found maybe a dozen people around where we were, taking photographs and asking if I'd sign autographs for them.

She had no idea what was going on.

'Who are they?'

I explained that they were just people from Cork, Tipperary and Wexford… and they were asking if they could have their picture taken with me.

'Just because of the hurling,' I said.

'What's hurling?'

So, I explained to her what hurling was and told her that I used to play.

'Right. You've never mentioned it.'

AFTER MY LAST match for Loughgiel, it was six years before I went to another game. It just wasn't a part of my life.

I was working in the shop and the music had gotten really busy since I stopped playing hurling. Dad dying affected me too. He was all about hurling. He was where I got my love for it from and when he was gone, I just didn't feel the same about the game.

Even though I played out my last season with the club, I didn't have the same enthusiasm. When I stopped playing it was worse because I was always a bad spectator.

If I was injured or rested – or worse, dropped – for a match I'd get agitated sitting on the bench, thinking I should be out there. To not be involved at all, just standing outside the wire like everyone else, would have been hard... too hard.

Nothing in particular made me go back.

I just woke up one day and decided it was time. I'd probably thought about it for a couple of years but couldn't give myself the kick up the backside I needed to go. Loughgiel were playing Rossa in the championship in Dunloy, and I went over on my own and stood where the Loughgiel supporters always stood in Dunloy.

Because Loughgiel supporters stood there, Dunloy people called it... 'Ill-bred hill'. It lived up to his name. I couldn't believe some of the stuff that was shouted. But I found myself wanting to shout stuff too.

A Dunloy player made a bad tackle and I couldn't help it.

'YOU DIRTY...'

I heard myself shouting all sorts of things. At the start of the match, I couldn't believe what I was hearing, and now I was hearing it from myself.

I had to move away and watch the match by myself. I didn't want someone looking over and thinking... *God, it was Niall Patterson who shouted that.*

Now, if we were playing Dunloy, I'd go over and stand on the Dunloy side, on the 20-metre line, often with Martin Brogan, who kept goals for Dunloy... and we would have a nice chat and watch the match.

I'd still be shouting for Loughgiel, but it's better for me to be away from the middle of the crowd. It can get very heated. Don't get me wrong, I can get very heated too, but I'm getting too old for a lot of that.

AS WELL AS being a supporter, I got back involved in the club coaching the goalkeepers. Since I had retired, I was asked a few times by different people to throw my hat into the ring to be part of a management team, but it wasn't something I ever thought about doing.

But our goalkeeper at the time, DD Quinn, asked me if I could work with him on some things when big matches were coming up. That turned into working with all the club's goalkeepers and I was surprised how much I enjoyed it.

The game had changed so much since I played that I knew I'd need to build up my knowledge if I was going to be of any use. So, I rang round the inter-county goalkeepers at that time – the late 2000s – and asked if I could pick their brains. The journalist Christy O'Connor gave me a lot of their phone numbers, but when it came to the man who was the gold standard for how a goalkeeper thought about the game back then – Cork's Dónal Óg Cusack – Christy warned me not to expect a lot.

I rang Dónal Óg and told him what I was doing, and that I didn't want to know any big secrets. Just one drill or idea would be great.

He sent up diagrams, plans for drills… all sorts of things. He was brilliant.

'If you need anything else, Niall… just pick up the phone!'

'Sambo' and 'Woody' took over the Antrim job in 2006 and had been at me for a couple of years to come on board and coach the goalkeepers. I told them that between the music and the shop, I just didn't have time.

Then, in 2009 with Antrim moving into the Leinster Championship, they wore me down.

So, a few months before the championship, I started to work with the 'keepers. It was a couple of nights a week. I drove my own car to training and didn't take any expenses. I did it because I enjoyed it. I wanted to help my county, and because 'Sambo' and 'Woody' had asked me to.

So as the match against Dublin was coming up, I went to the county board and asked for a ticket.

'Absolutely. And this is what it'll cost you!'

Get me an expenses sheet and we'll see how many tickets that's worth, I thought.

When 'Woody' found out I had paid for a ticket, he told me to tell the county board I had changed my mind, wasn't going, and wanted my money back. 'Woody' gave me one of his tickets and one of the players from Loughgiel, Johnny Campbell, gave me another.

'Sambo' told me to come down to the hotel before the match and travel to Croke Park on the bus with the team. It was the first time I been there since Kilkenny in 1991. Everything had changed, the stands, the changing room… but when I got out onto the pitch itself, I felt like I was 16 again and in the old stadium for the first time.

Or playing there for Antrim or Loughgiel. That feeling was exactly the same.

AFTER WE WON in 1989, Loughgiel didn't reach another Antrim final for 14 years. Then they lost six in-a-row.

Before the 2010 season, 'Beaver' McCarry came to me and said he was going for the manager's job and he wanted me and Sean Carey – 'Tinkle' – to come along with him.

I had loved working with DD and the goalkeepers but management was different, it was nearly a full-time job.

I had a chat with Naomi and she told me if I wanted to give it a go, then I should go ahead… do it for a year and get it out of my system, because it was obvious to her I had gotten to the stage where I wanted to do something like this. I decided that if we got the job, I'd give it everything for a year, seven nights a week if I had to, but if we didn't get it that would be me. I wouldn't think about it again.

We went down to the club and we met with the interview panel selecting the manager.

'What do you think you can do for this club, Niall?'

Yous have short memories, I thought to myself.

I said I lived for the club and I thought I could pass on some of the knowledge I had picked up from the great managers I had played under for club and county.

Our biggest problem was losing county finals – and losing them in every way you could imagine. Something needed to change. There were a couple of lads who had retired, but still well capable of contributing something, with the sort of know-how we maybe needed to push us over the edge.

We suggested bringing them in, in July, ahead of the championship, and training them for two or three months, just to be subs… to be there if we needed them. If we're playing Cushendall and leading by two points with 10 minutes to go and under the cosh, and you can bring these two boys on to steady the ship and win a championship, why wouldn't you?

It was a non-starter. If you didn't train every single night, from the start of January, then it didn't matter if you could be the difference between winning a championship final – which was supposed to be the be-and end-all.

I was one hundred percent confident we could have helped those players win an Antrim championship, but we never got the chance.

Whether or not we could have helped them win an All-Ireland, I'm not sure. PJ O'Mullan's son PJ junior got the job and brought Jim Nelson in as the coach.

The rest is history. Loughgiel finally won the Antrim title again in 2010... and in 2012 won the All-Ireland.

I don't regret it, and in 2012 when DD Quinn and Johnny Campbell captained Loughgiel to the same All-Ireland title I had in 1983, there wasn't a prouder Shamrock in Croke Park than me.

I TOOK RHIANNON and Sharelle to the 2012 final.

They were only 11 and 12 at the time, and made their way through the turnstile with me behind them. But I couldn't get in. There had been a ticket mix-up and they had two Cusack Stand tickets, but for some reason mine was for the Hogan.

So, I started to panic that they'd wander off and get lost in Croke Park, the first time they'd ever been to a hurling match there.

Conor O'Donovan, who was the Tipperary full-back in 1989, saw me and said hello, probably wondering why I was in a panic? I told him what had happened and Conor went and got someone and made sure I got in, and was reunited with the girls.

Some Tipp men are all right after all.

It was a special feeling to see Loughgiel win that day. The fact the girls were there made it even better. That's what clubs are about – family connections and friends and community. I stood in Croke Park and cried like a baby.

I consider myself so lucky to have been able to do that as a player and then to be able to see it as a supporter, and it's something I wouldn't begrudge any club. When I tell people that, they say to me, 'You mean to tell me you'd like to see Dunloy win the All-Ireland?'

'Of course!'

Now, I want Loughgiel to beat them any time they play them, but Dunloy people love their parish and their club every bit as much as Loughgiel people do. Dunloy lost four All-Ireland finals and I can honestly say I wanted them to win all of them.

When I was younger, I thought Loughgiel was special because of how obsessed we are with hurling, but I soon found out it's the same in Dunloy or Cushendall... in every club at their own level.

I've been down in Cushendall playing in the bars on the nights they came back from winning the championship, and the buzz was unbelievable. Every club should get to experience that.

Of course, even if Dunloy or Cushendall won 10 All-Irelands each, they'll never take away from the fact that we did it first... and we did it for Loughgiel.

WHEN PEOPLE PICK their best-ever Antrim side, or their best-ever Loughgiel side, my name sometimes gets mentioned and, to be honest, I'm bit embarrassed by it. I just went out and tried to do my best for myself and my teammates.

I loved playing for Loughgiel beside life-long friends... and I loved playing for Antrim, with more friends and with the pride that comes with playing for your county. I've never understood a hurler not wanting to play for his county. If you think anything at all of yourself as a player, you want to put yourself against the best and see how you stand against them, and that means playing county hurling.

I never got to the very top, but I was fit to challenge to be the best, to play against the best and to reach that level.

When it came to Loughgiel and Antrim, I just happened to be the best in that position at that time. Maybe people would disagree... and I wouldn't argue.

All I can say is that when I was handed the shirt, I tried to do my best every time. After Loughgiel won the All-Ireland in 2012 there was a lot of talk around the club asking which team was better. It's something to have a bit of banter about, but I don't think you'll ever get a straight answer comparing teams like that from different eras.

The 2012 team were playing a completely different game to the one we played. Even the game the 2012 team played doesn't much look like the one being played 10 years later. The game has changed. and so have the teams that play it.

One thing no one can argue with is that the 2012 team had some spirit. Most of those players had lost six finals in-a-row. To go through that and then win four in-a-row themselves, and an All-Ireland as well, showed serious character. They had some great players too, but so did our 1983 team.

Many people would say Liam 'Winker' Watson, who scored 3-7 in the All-Ireland final and 16 points in the semi-final, is Loughgiel's best ever player, and I wouldn't dispute that because he's a fabulous hurler... but we had some fabulous hurlers on our team as well.

His uncle Brendan Laverty was our 'Winker'. Match after match in our All-Ireland season he was the man who got the crucial scores, who you knew you could trust to come up trumps.

A Brendan Laverty in the modern game would do every bit as much damage as his nephew, and the way he could score goals would make him an even bigger nightmare for defenders than he was back then.

After we won the All-Ireland, people compared us to the great Loughgiel team of the 60s – the legends I had been lucky enough to watch training and playing, and who I had heard story after story about when I was growing up. If you asked anyone round Loughgiel who remembered that team what they were like, you'd soon find out the esteem they were held in. Neil McMullan, who took over from my father at full-back and was his life-long friend, and his brother Seamus in the half-back line, were legends in defence.

You couldn't give away a free within 90 yards, or Seamus would step up and knock it over the bar. And you really didn't want to be facing one of his penalties – because you wouldn't stop it.

Arthur Connolly was a massive player with Seamus in the half-back line, and Dan Gillan was the perfect midfielder for the way that team played. The midfield needed to keep the ball moving and, whether it was on the ground or in the air, Dan never missed a ball.

Everybody talked about the half-forward line of Barney Campbell, Seamus Richmond and Brendan McGarry. They reckoned it was the best half-forward line ever in Antrim. Wee Barney did all the spade-work, and Seamus and Brendan got all the scores. By the time I came into the seniors a lot of that great team had retired, but I was lucky to get to play with Brendan and Seamus, and they were still on the panel when we won the All-Ireland in 1983.

I've already mentioned Seamus' influence on my hurling, my music and my life, but Brendan helped me a lot when I came into the senior side. Johnny Coyle was my hero and taught me the fundamentals of goalkeeping, but goalkeepers can learn just as much from a great forward. *Know your enemy.*

Brendan was one of the best forwards we ever had, and when I was just in the team and still a teenager he would take me down to the pitch before training started and put me through my paces, showing me what way a forward would strike balls, how they'd come at you, how a forward thinks and what they're trying to do.

We were blessed in our club with players like Brendan McGarry, Seamus Richmond, Johnny Coyle and so many others.

And I was blessed to play with them and learn from them.

IT'S JUST AS well I didn't meet Naomi until after I had finished playing. After I explained to her what hurling was and showed her as well, she was clear about it.

'We wouldn't have been going out. I couldn't have stood and watched that… far too rough.'

I was trying to explain to her that it's not a rough game. It's a hard game, but you're taught when you're young how to protect yourself and it's not as dangerous as it maybe looks with the sticks flying about.

I'm not sure how much I managed to sway her, but a trip up to meet Ger Rogan in Belfast swung things in the other direction. 'Rogie' was based up in Casement Park making sticks at the time and he met Naomi, and we got talking about old matches.

'Rogie' being *'Rogie'*, he was getting into it and going on about killing this and killing that, and doing damage all round him.

For God's sake, 'Rogie', shut up, I thought.

We got back in the car and Naomi turned to me.

'Aye, it's not a rough game!'

'That's just 'Rogie'… he *kills* all round him in his head!'

I don't think I won the argument.

SOMETHING NAOMI DID find out about great friends like 'Rogie' and other people I'd met through hurling, is that there really is something special about the bonds the GAA creates. We took a trip down to Birr and the car broke down about 500 yards from the hotel. So, we got our bags and headed to the hotel to get checked in, and get someone to have a look at the car. In the hotel, we met Dinny Cahill and his wife Marian.

Dinny was asking what had happened and, when I told him the car had broken down, straightaway he told me his son had a company car I could use and he'd bring it over in the morning. I thanked Dinny but told him we already had something sorted.

'He was only being nice!' said Naomi after he had gone.

'No, he really meant it.'

The following morning, Dinny rang and said, 'Niall, we can head over with this car for you now?'

I had to politely decline again. We were okay, I said.

Then we met Pat Cleary in the hotel and the second he found out what had happened to the car, he was offering one himself as well. Naomi got a little peek at what being in the GAA means on that trip.

She didn't know at the time, but one of the best holidays we ever had, not long after we started going out, was thanks to hurling. We called into Joe Connolly's shop in Galway and he helped us plan a great time travelling round the county for the next week.

Joe was one of the few players from outside Ulster I played against, who I got to know a little bit. It's something I regret – not that I was looking for any big friendships, but more that it would have been nice to just chat with these great players I admired. It's not in my nature to put myself forward like that.

I have a group of friends who I enjoy going out with and I could sit and talk to anybody, but I would be a bit of a loner that way with people I don't know.

When I was out in New York playing with Offaly, it was all about socialising. You played your match, you went to the bar and you drank. Boys would be up buying you drinks because you were over from Ireland, but I didn't drink… so I'd have passed myself for about an hour and headed back.

There were stories in the press talking about how much of a character I was and it was a load of rubbish – they never met me. They weren't saying I was doing anything bad, but they had me painted as a bit of a party animal, that I enjoyed a drink and all that… probably because I played in a band.

I PLAYED MY match and headed home.

There were goalkeepers I probably should have gotten to know and talk to, but I kept myself to myself. Damien Martin won two All-Irelands with Offaly and kept goals for St Rynagh's against us in the All-Ireland final. He's a lovely man and actually ended up working with my brother Anthony.

There was one year that I couldn't get an All-Ireland final ticket, and Anthony rang Damien and I had a ticket the next day. Apart from Damien, John Commins was the only goalkeeper outside Ulster I really spoke to and got friendly with.

Looking back, I should have made an effort to talk to someone like Ken Hogan after the All-Ireland final and get to know him a little bit, as well as other goalkeepers I played against a lot. Just to be able to have a wee chat when we ran into each other or after a match, to talk about goalkeeping.

Part of the problem is that I didn't put myself on the same level as them boys. When I was finished a game, I shook hands and away I went. I put those boys on pedestals.

I wanted to get away because at the time I didn't think I should be even on the same pitch as someone like Ken Hogan. I was probably doing myself a disservice, because we had earned our place on the field with those players and those teams.

Facebook has meant I've been able to correct that a little, and now I can chat and catch up with boys I played against 30 or 40 years ago. I can even troll them – even if I don't mean it. Every so often the semi-final against Offaly pops up in some way on Facebook and – of course – I'll share it.

Regular as clockwork, Daithi Regan will reply. 'Why do you keep sharing that, Niall? What are you doing to me!'

THE GREAT MEMORIES of that day come with the sadness that Danny and James McNaughton and Jim Nelson have passed away.

Danny was only 40 when he took unwell while he was playing a match with Cushendall in Dunloy. He came off, but collapsed and died there at the side of the pitch. His brother James was just 51 when he passed 18 years later.

They were both great men to be around and both great men to have at your side. We all came from clubs who were fierce rivals, but the atmosphere in the Antrim panel through all those years really did feel like a family, and it wasn't just among the players.

If we were down in Cushendall training, Danny's wife Anne-Marie, James' wife Ann and Fergus McNaughton's wife Maureen looked after us like we were their own. You couldn't turn around without another cup of tea or a sandwich coming your way. It was a wee thing, but it said a lot about the sort of people we had in the team and around the team.

Danny was a born winner. If I didn't puck the ball out to Danny, after the game he would have come in and ate the face off me. He wanted the ball all the time – he wanted to contribute to the team all the time.

Danny and Leonard McKeegan were cousins and at Antrim training you couldn't have put your finger between their shoulders. They'd be side by side, joined at the hip around the pitch, neither wanting to let the other win a ball off them. It was dad who first pointed it out to me.

'See those two boys there? That's what *will to win* is – and that is what every one of us needs to be like.'

James McNaughton was a class act, one of the best hurlers Antrim ever produced, and great craic too. Cushendall were playing Ballycastle in a Feis Cup final in Cushendall the week before Antrim were due to play Down in the Ulster final. Some of the Down boys were up watching and I was along with 'Woody', 'Cloot' and 'Beaver'.

James was over chatting with us before the match and we were telling him, 'You behave yourself out there, we've got an Ulster final coming up'.

'Och, sure, it's just a Feis Cup… I'll be all right!'

James was on Olcan Laverty and when the first ball came in, he went through him.

'Here we go!' said 'Woody'. 'The wires have been touched.'

After the match, James just laughed.

'Och, sure you know yourself. Once the game's on… you take no prisoners!'

BEFORE THE ALL-IRELAND final, we sang *We are Jim Nelson's Men* – and we really were.

The 1989 team had been in the making for nearly a decade, but it's no coincidence that we made the breakthrough under Jim. People like Gilly McIlhatton and my dad had done their bit in the years before, and Sean McGuinness pushed us further when he came in, but it was Jim who brought us into Division One… into an All-Ireland final, and very nearly into a couple more.

As well as the Antrim seniors, he managed the county camogie team to an All-Ireland junior title and laid the foundations for the Rossa camogs to win a senior All-Ireland. And no one in Loughgiel will ever forgot what he did to help the club win the All-Ireland in 2012. If someone proposed building a statue of him in the village, I doubt you'd find many dissenting voices.

I can't think of any other Belfast man you could say that about.

He contributed so much by managing teams at all levels in hurling and camogie in Antrim, and you could go all over the county and hear hundreds of different people tell hundreds of different stories about Jim and the sort of man he was.

He turned us into a band of brothers with Antrim.

A *Field of Brothers*!

And I'm sure he did the same everywhere else he went. Bands of brothers and sisters – hurling and camogie families – all thanks to Jim Nelson.

WE SHARED SOME great times off the pitch as well as on it.

A couple of times when we were playing down in Kerry, we flew instead of taking a bus. The first plane might as well have been a bus – it was like a transit van with two ironing boards sticking out the sides. 'Woody' especially enjoyed that journey – he was on the verge of passing out all the way down to Kerry.

The next time we flew, we flew in style. There was cabin crew and everything – and everything including drink on the way back.

Anyone could make the most of it and, when we landed back at Aldergrove late at night, the spirits were high. As we were walking through the airport, one of the players was twirling his stick, but didn't notice a sign hanging above the corridor.

Smack went the stick against the sign, down came the sign… smack went the sign onto his head. Blood everywhere. Then, no one could find our kit.

Then, we went on to a nearby hotel for our meal, which the boys all enjoyed – except the one who ended up face first in his dinner… passed out. That was the end of drink on the plane.

Just because I was a non-drinker didn't mean I couldn't get stories told about me – although 'Sambo' told one in his autobiography that needs to be set straight.

AFTER THE ALL-IRELAND year, we went out to Portugal for a training trip. I was sharing a room with 'Woody' and 'Cloot'… and it was my turn to cook. I went down to the shop, but everything was in Portuguese.

I saw a big bottle with something yellow in it, and a picture of what looked like a chip pan on the label. *Okay,* I thought, *this must be cooking oil.*

I brought it back up to the room, filled the pan and turned on the heat. But after a few minutes, I started to suspect there was something wrong – it wasn't behaving like cooking oil. It was then I realised it was washing up liquid.

According to those boys – and 'Sambo's' book – the place was a mess, covered in bubbles, but that never happened. Fake news… though it didn't stop John Carson, who was down by the pool, with 'Cloot' and 'Woody' sitting next to him, shouting up… 'Niall! Have you those chips washed yet?!'

His tall-tales about me aside, 'Sambo' was as good a man as you could ever ask to be on your team. He was good hurler, but wouldn't have had as much ability as other boys in the team. His son Shane, who played for Antrim and helped Cushendall reach the All-Ireland final in 2016, was your typical classy, skilful, talented hurler.

'Sambo' was different. He just wouldn't give up, and was a real inspiration who could lift everyone around him. He won an All Star at midfield, but for me he was a perfect left half-back. The Cushendall half-back line he played on, with Leonard McKeegan and James McNaughton, was the best I ever played against.

'Sambo' was the boy who put the hand up, Leonard was the boy who broke the ball down, James was the boy who did the sweeping.

Thankfully, when we were playing down in Cushendall, I could put most of my puckouts into the square as their pitch back then was so small. If we were at our place or another pitch, we'd try hitting the midfield because that half back-line was nearly unbeatable and was what Cushendall built their success on.

A half-back sticking their hand up and catching a puckout or a ball out of defence lifts a team, and *lifts* supporters like nothing else. It's a change in momentum, a burst of excitement that is a rarer occurrence in the game now that teams build from the back and try to play through the lines.

The year Loughgiel finally won the county title after losing all those finals, we had our backs against the wall against Cushendall. We were in the lead but they kept coming at us and Martin Scullion caught two balls in our half-back line in the dying moments of the game. Our supporters nearly took the roof off the Casement Park stand when he made those catches, and we held on.

That's what 'Sambo' gave you.

He'd stick the hand up, with six boys flailing all round him, and he'd come out of that with blood pouring from his head… but the ball safely in his hand.

I'VE LOST COUNT of how many times I've seen the 1989 All-Ireland semi-final. We watched it when we got back up from Dublin when we were still celebrating, and any time it comes on somewhere, it's hard for me not to at least have a look.

It was a day to remember and to relive.

It took me nearly 32 years to bring myself to watch the 1989 All-Ireland final. From the moment I let Declan Ryan's shot get past me, I kept it with me. Being able to get back on the pitch against Cork at Croke Park and show my worth at that level again helped, but only a little... and only briefly.

I carried it with me until I stopped playing.

I carried it with me every day since. I didn't dwell on anything else that happened when I played – as a goalkeeper, you'd drive yourself mad if you did – but I could never shake the All-Ireland final.

We had been hammered and I had had a stinker.

I didn't need to see it again to know that. After the match, and the years since, people came up to me and told me I had a good final. I would listen and smile and say 'thanks', but all the while I was thinking... *What game were you watching?*

I just thought they were being nice and I didn't need that. As far as I was concerned, I had let the team down... and I'd let myself down.

THE GIRLS WERE all away and I had the house to myself on a Saturday, so I settled down to watch Antrim play Dublin, and Laois play Wexford, in the 2021 Leinster Championship. It was a disappointing loss for an Antrim team who had had a great league, and then Wexford beat Laois pulling up.

Flicking round the channels I saw that another match was going to be shown... the 1989 All-Ireland final. I don't know why, but I thought...

Right, it's time. I'm going to watch this.

I stopped for a second, about to change my mind, then decided to go through with it. I'm not sure why. Maybe the same reason people will sit through a horror film. That's what it had always been in mind.

My own personal horror film... playing in my head for 30 years.

As I watched, I saw things I must have forgotten by the next day. So much of it was new to me. Declan Ryan's goal was horribly familiar. But then, as I kept watching, I realised that that wasn't the whole story.

It was still the turning point in the match when Tipp kicked on and left us in their wake, but despite what I had thought all those years – and despite what other people had tried to tell me – it was the *only* mistake I made.

I couldn't do anything about their other goals, and we were outclassed all over the pitch. It was clear to see. That was Tipp's day, they grabbed their chance and we couldn't live with them.

For more than 40 years, if you'd have asked me, I would have told you that losing to Wexford in the Leinster minor semi-final was the biggest single disappointment of my playing career. That probably would have sounded strange when I went on to lose in a senior All-Ireland final, but as far as I was concerned it was true.

In my mind, I was gutted after Tipperary beat us in 1989, but mainly because of my own performance. I had made a bad mistake and we ended up being hammered, but that disappointment was drawn out. The game against Tipp was over long before full-time. The disappointment had time to build and we had time to get used to it. Long before the end, it had sunk in that we weren't going to win the All-Ireland.

The disappointment in the Wexford game came all of a sudden. That's why we were sitting in the changing room with our heads in our hands for an hour. We had lost the thing in a blur at the end of the match. We didn't know what had hit us.

But sitting watching that All-Ireland final again didn't just jog my memory about what had happened that day, it reminded how I felt. Maybe by not thinking about it, I was protecting myself from those feelings... or maybe it was the enormity of the All-Ireland final itself that made my mind play tricks.

Before the match, Michael O'Grady had tried to let us know what to expect. He told us he had worked with teams in All-Ireland finals before and he talked to players after the match and they couldn't remember a thing that had happened in it. I couldn't believe that.

How can you play in an All-Ireland final and not remember it?

But it happened to me.

Losing that final was devastating. It's the biggest day in hurling – a hundred times bigger than any other. Of course, the disappointment is massive, there's no way around it.

But I was still glad I watched it again, and it did me far more good than harm. For years the biggest hurling *What if?* had been rattling around in my head.

What if I hadn't let in that goal?

We might not have won, but if I just stuck up my hand and caught that ball, who knows what would have happened?

There was only three points in it. Nothing.

Every day since that final, I honestly thought it was something I would take to my grave.

But sitting at home in Cloughmills, by the time the final whistle went – after Nicky English's bullet hit my net and the Tipp crowd surged past me onto the pitch – I could sit back and look at that day in a whole new light.

I was so glad I watched it.

It lifted the burden I had carried all those years.

I slept well that night.

Epilogue

IT'S DECEMBER 2020, the strangest time you could imagine.

We're in between lockdowns as the world battles against a coronavirus pandemic that has turned it upside down. One of the strange things is that, even though it's December, Antrim are about to play at Croke Park on All-Ireland final day… for the first time since we did in 1989.

The pandemic pushed the GAA championships into winter, and kept supporters out of great stadiums like Nowlan Park, Thurles and Croke Park itself. Antrim are playing on the big day, but it's not the big match.

Before Limerick play Waterford for the MacCarthy Cup, Antrim play Kerry for the Joe McDonagh Cup and the right to be back among the big boys in 2021. It's not the same, but with all of Antrim hurling's ups and – mostly – downs over the years, it's still a time when there's a bit of excitement about the county team.

I'm in Dunloy, over getting bread for my mum at 'Pappy's', the O'Kane family bakery started by the uncle of my old teammate Gary – now one of the Antrim selectors.

I run into another old teammate, Brian Donnelly, out on his bicycle. His son Matthew will be the Antrim full-back at Croke Park against Kerry. Hard to get around. Something every goalkeeper wants in his full-back.

We stop and talk, as we always do when we run into each other, and Brian tells me he can see the same comradeship that we had in this Antrim team of

Matthew's. *Maybe that's why they're doing well, and why they'll end up winning on Sunday.*

Maybe that's why in our day we could do well. We're still the best of mates, that whole 1989 team. The boys suited and booted… in our saffron ties on county final day 30 years later, are still great, *great* friends.

Brian reminds me of the time I broke that stick across his chest in the McMullan Cup. How when all of us hurled against each other with our clubs we never took a backward step, but once we started playing together with the county – from minors right on through to when we retired – we always stood together… ready to take anything any team was going to hit us with.

When we were teenagers and started playing together on Antrim under-16 and minor teams, our shop in Cloughmills was where we used to meet up to get the bus. Once everyone landed, we'd go out to the side of the shop and batter the ball against the wall… waiting for the bus to arrive to take us to training or a match.

We always hoped the bus would be late, so we could get just five more minutes playing together.

When we arrived down at the Grand Hotel in Malahide before the All-Ireland senior final, we piled out of the bus and into the grounds, like we always did… with sticks and balls, to puck around for as long as we could before the staff lost their patience with us.

Even just for five minutes.

A team of friends… a field of brothers. Playing together.

MORE
GREAT
SPORTS BOOKS
FROM
HERO BOOKS

'A Game that Smiles'
Richie Bennis: An Autobiography

RICHIE BENNIS IS one of the true legends remaining in the game of hurling. A towering figure in Limerick GAA, he played a central role as the county won the All-Ireland title in 1973 and then he strived as hard as anyone to see the Liam MacCarthy Cup return to the Treaty County.

It was a wait of 45 years – during which time Bennis worked at grassroots hurling in the famed Patrickswell club, where he hurled into his 40s and won 10 county titles. He also led Limerick as team manager to the 2007 All-Ireland final where they lost to Kilkenny.

In 2018, Limerick were crowned All-Ireland champions.

For Richie Bennis, a long agonising wait ended. His story is one of triumph, and heartache and personal tragedy, and a courage that was never dimmed.

Authors: Richie Bennis with Ciarán Kennedy
Hardback: €25.00
Paperback: €20.00
Ebook: €9.99
ISBN: 9781910827093

Buy on **Amazon**
(and paperback available in all good bookstores)

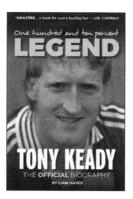

One Hundred and Ten Percent Legend
Tony Keady: The Official Biography

WHEN TONY KEADY died suddenly in August of 2017, at just 53 years of age, a whole county mourned and the rest of the country stopped in its tracks to say goodbye to a legend of the game of hurling.

In 1988, after leading Galway to a second All-Ireland title in succession, he was crowned the greatest hurler in Ireland. He was 25 years of age and there was nobody like him, nobody to touch him in the maroon No.6 shirt. But, four years later, and still not 30, after being wrongly banned for 12 months by the GAA, he was also discarded by his own county and refused a maroon jersey the very last time he walked out onto Croke Park behind the Galway team.

A few months before his death, Tony Keady visited Liam Hayes and told him he wished to tell his own story. He felt it was time, but tragically time was not on Tony's side. Tony's wife Margaret and his daughter Shannon and his three boys Anthony, Harry and Jake, decided to finish telling the story of a father and a hurler who always asked those around him for '110%'.

Author: Liam Hayes
Hardback: €25.00
Paperback: €20.00
Ebook: €9.99
ISBN: 9781910827048

Buy on **Amazon**
(and paperback available in all good bookstores)

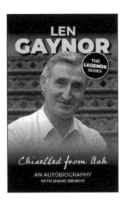

Chiselled from Ash
Len Gaynor: An Autobiography

CHISELLED FROM ASH is a story of love and honour.

It's the story of Len Gaynor's great love for the game of hurling, and how he has honoured the great game his whole life.

Len Gaynor won it all with Tipperary, finishing his career with three All-Ireland hurling titles, four Munster titles and two National League titles in the 1960s and 70s. But the flamboyant wing back also wanted to give back at the end of his career.

The Kilruane MacDonaghs clubman – and winner of three county titles – quickly proved himself to be one of the smartest and most ambitious coaches in the game. At club level he strived to teach and help the next generation, and led his own Kilruane and neighbouring clubs to success – and at county level through the 1990s Len Gaynor managed Tipperary and Clare on the biggest stages in the game.

Authors: Len Gaynor with Shane Brophy
Hardback: €25.00
Paperback: €20.00
Ebook: €9.99
ISBN: 9781910827208

Buy on **Amazon**
(and paperback available in all good bookstores)

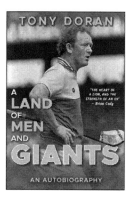

A Land of Men and Giants
The Tony Doran Autobiography

WEXFORD'S ALL-IRELAND winning hero Tony Doran was a giant in the game of hurling through the 1960s, 70s and 80s, at a time when full-forwards were ordered to plunder goals. In his 19 years and 187 appearances as a Wexford hurler, Tony Doran successfully went for goal 131 times. But Doran also played against giants from Kilkenny, Tipperary and Cork, and so many other counties, at a time when the game of hurling tested the wits and the courage of every man on the field.

Some of these men became giants.

A Land of Men and Giants is the story told by Tony Doran of a life spent living and competing against legendary men and true giants of the game.

A Land of Men and Giants: The Autobiography of Tony Doran is edited by award-winning writer and author Liam Hayes.

Authors: Tony Doran with Liam Hayes
Hardback: €25.00
Paperback: €20.00
Ebook: €9.99
ISBN: 9781910827031

Buy on **Amazon**
(and paperback available in all good bookstores)

CORK HURLING
GAME OF MY LIFE

25 OF THE GREATEST CORK hurlers over the last 60 years remember the one game in their careers that defined their sporting lives.

Including: Gerald McCarthy, Tony Maher, Brian Murphy, Martin Coleman, Tom Cashman, Ger Cunningham, John Fenton, Johnny Crowley, Jimmy Barry-Murphy, John Considine, Ger Fitzgerald, Tony O'Sullivan, Tomás Mulcahy, Seán O'Gorman, Denis Walsh, Seánie McGrath, Ronan Curran, Wayne Sherlock, Kieran Murphy, Tom Kenny, Shane O'Neill, Ben O'Connor, Stephen McDonnell, Anthony Nash, Daniel Kearney.

A game that will live with each person forever.

Author: Denis Hurley
Hardback: €25.00
Paperback: €20.00
Ebook: €9.99
ISBN: 9781910827451

Buy on **Amazon**
(and paperback available in all good bookstores)

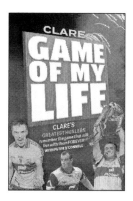

CLARE
GAME OF MY LIFE

30 OF THE GREATEST CLARE hurlers over the last 60 years remember the one game in their careers that defined their sporting lives.

Including: Naoise Jordan, Jackie O'Gorman, Seamus Durack, Sean O'Hehir, Colm Honan, Sean Stack, Tommy Keane, Tommy Guilfoyle, David Forde, Ollie Baker, Stephen McNamara, Frank Lohan, Fergie Tuohy, Gerry McInerney, Fergal Hegarty, Ger Loughnane, Niall Gilligan, Gerry Quinn, Anthony Daly, Brian O'Connell, Fergal Lynch, Cian Dillon, Podge Collins, Brendan Bugler, Pat O'Connor, Colin Ryan, Patrick Donnellan, Conor Ryan, John Conlon and Tony Kelly

A game that will live with each person forever.

Author: Peter O'Connell
Hardback: €25.00
Paperback: €20.00
Ebook: €9.99
ISBN: 9781910827376

Buy on **Amazon**
(and paperback available in all good bookstores)

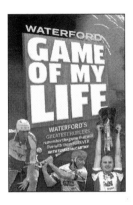

WATERFORD
GAME OF MY LIFE

25 OF THE GREATEST WATERFORD hurlers over the last 60 years remember the one game in their careers that defined their sporting lives.

Including: Tom Cunningham, Martin Óg Morrissey, Michael O'Connor, Larry Guinan, Jim Greene, Brian Greene, Patricia Jackman, Mossie Walsh, John Galvin, Shane Ahearne, Stephen Frampton, Fergal Hartley, Sean Cullinane, Brian Flannery, Eoin Murphy, John Mullane, Beth Carton , Paul Flynn , Dan Shanahan and Maurice Shanahan

A game that will live with each person forever.

Author: Tómas McCarthy
Hardback: €25.00
Paperback: €20.00
Ebook: €9.99
ISBN: 9781910827406

Buy on **Amazon**
(and paperback available in all good bookstores)

TIPPERARY
GAME OF MY LIFE

THE GREATEST TIPPERARY hurlers over the last 50 years remember the one game in blue and gold that defined their lives...

Including: Jimmy Finn, Theo English, Tony Wall, Tadhg O'Connor, Dinny Ryan, Babs Keating, John Sheedy, Ken Hogan, Colm Bonnar, Cormac Bonnar, Declan Carr, Michael Cleary, Pat Fox, Conal Bonnar, Declan Ryan, Michael Ryan, Joe Hayes, Eamonn Corcoran, Tommy Dunne, Shane McGrath, James Woodlock, Brendan Cummins, Eoin Kelly, Michael Cahill, Brendan Maher, James Barry, Seamus Callinan and more...

A game that will live with each person forever.

Author: Stephen Gleeson
Hardback: €25.00
Paperback: €20.00
Ebook: €9.99
ISBN: 9781910827185

Buy on **Amazon**
(and paperback available in all good bookstores)

GALWAY
GAME OF MY LIFE

TWENTY-FIVE OF GALWAY'S greatest hurlers remember the one game that will live with them forever...

Including: Jimmy Hegarty, Ned Dervan, Andy Fenton, Iggy Clarke, Sean Silke, Joe Connolly, PJ Molloy, Noel Lane, John Connolly, Mike Conneely, Anthony Cunningham, Pete Finnerty, Eanna Ryan, Gerry McInerney, John Commins, Michael Coleman, Micheál Donoghue, Padraig Kelly, Kevin Broderick, Ger Farragher, David Collins, Ollie Canning, Alan Kerins, Fergal Moore and Gearoid McInerney.

A game that will live with each person forever.

Author: Ollie Turner
Hardback: €25.00
Paperback: €20.00
Ebook: €9.99
ISBN: 9781910827284

Buy on **Amazon**
(and paperback available in all good bookstores)

Printed in Great Britain
by Amazon

13711853R00132